This Book Belongs to:

●●●

MMG PUBLISHING

Thank you for purchasing this book. If you enjoyed this title, feedback on Amazon would be greatly appreciated. If you had any issues, then please drop us an email via clunkable@gmail.com

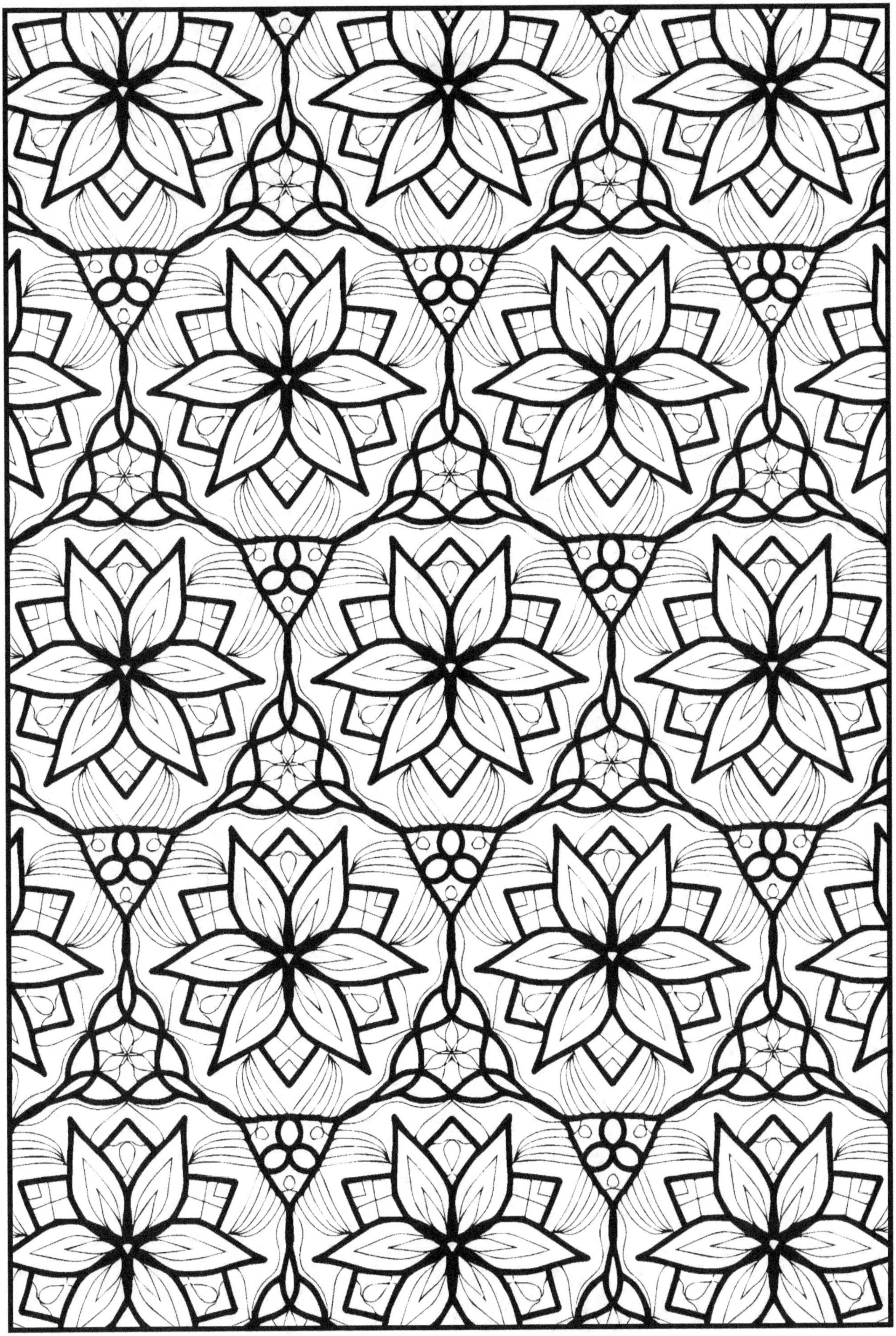

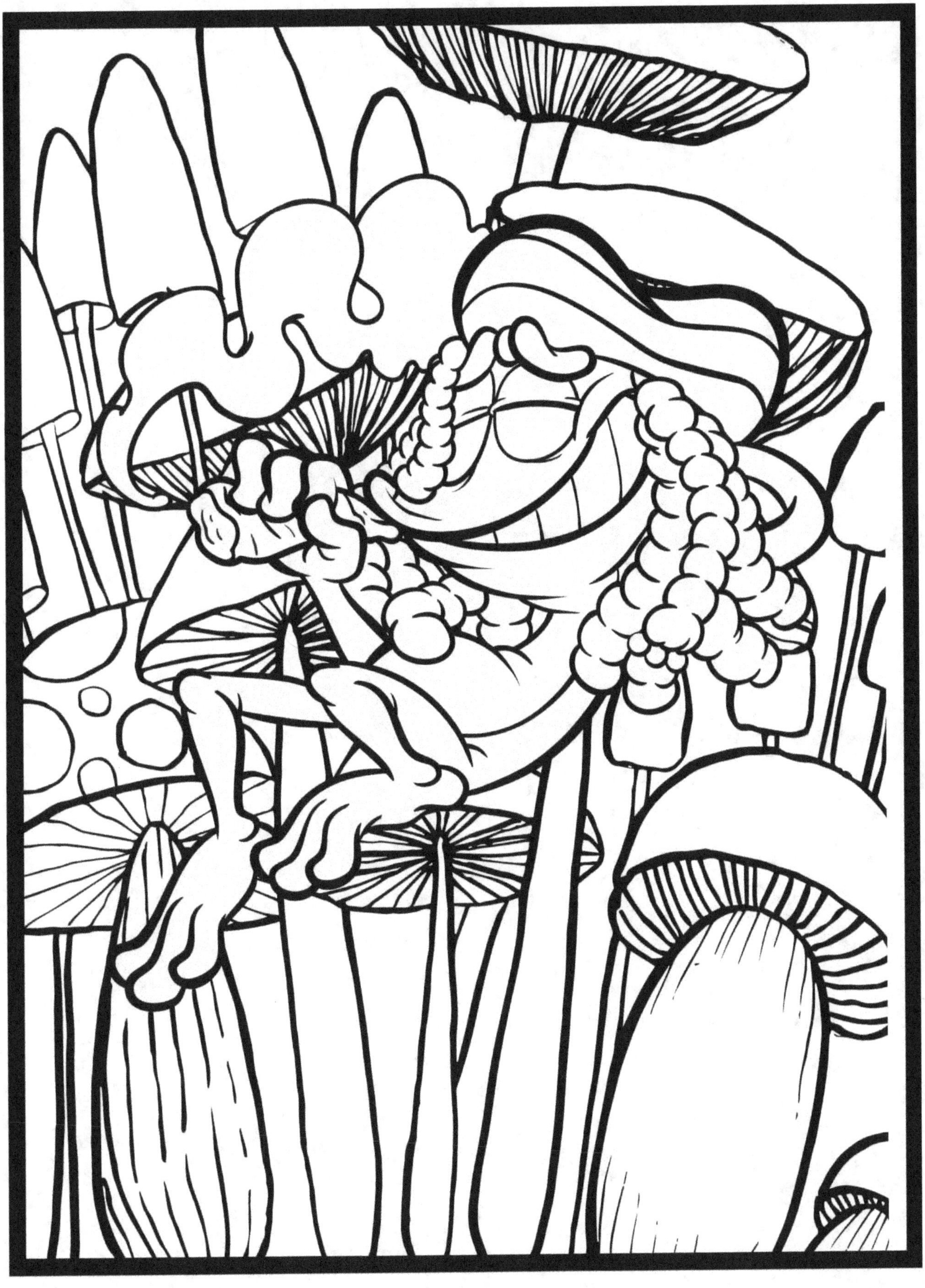

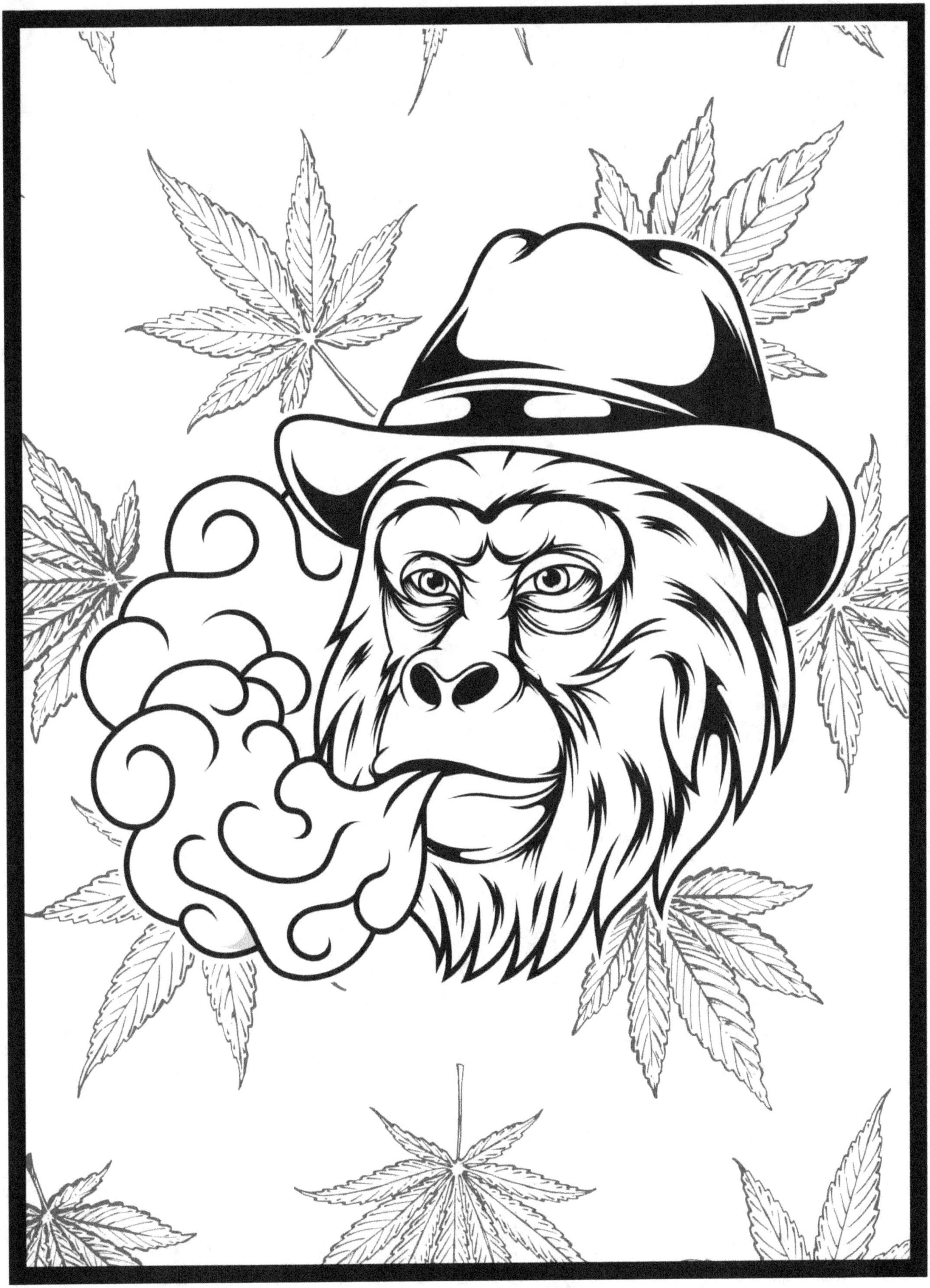

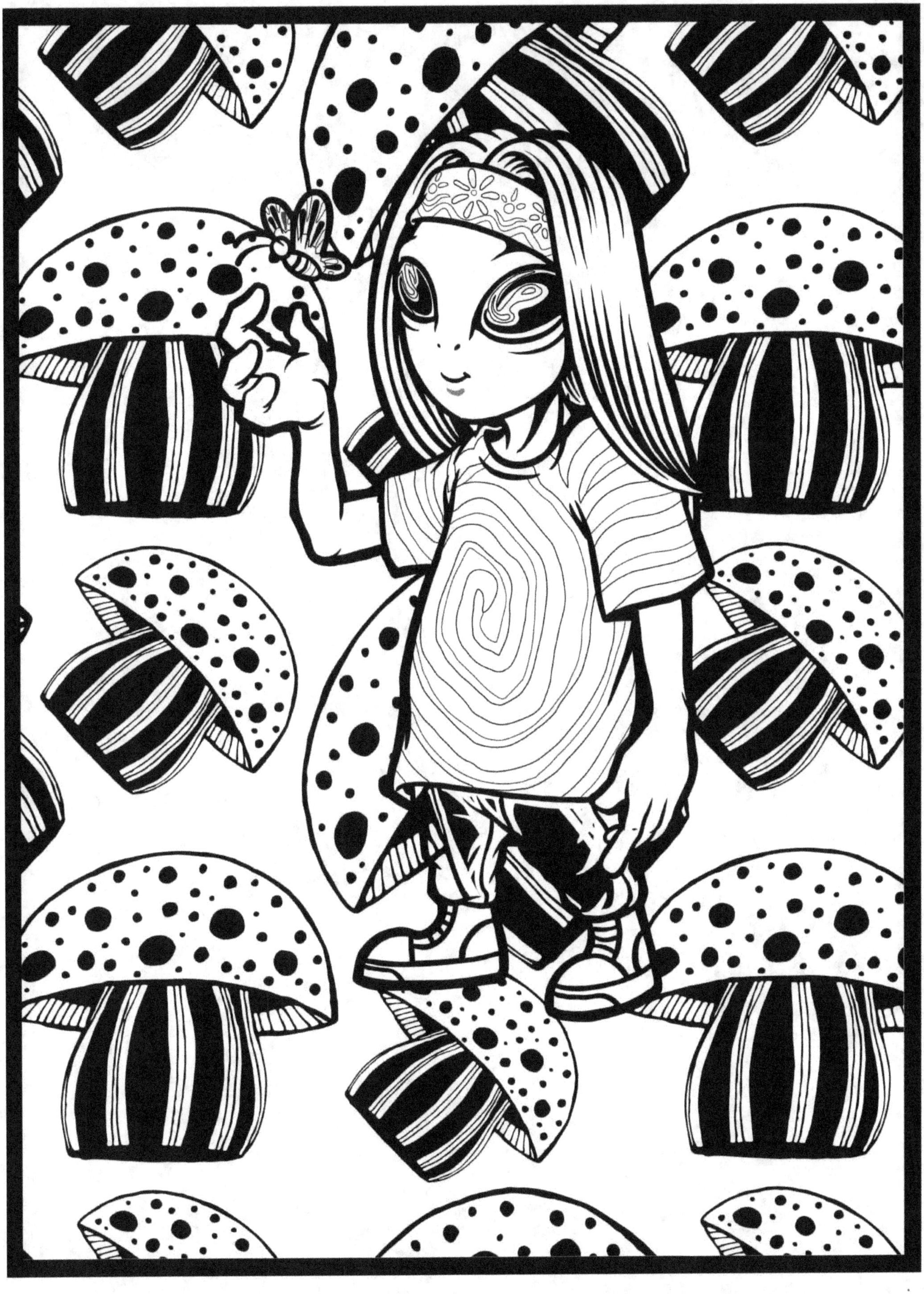

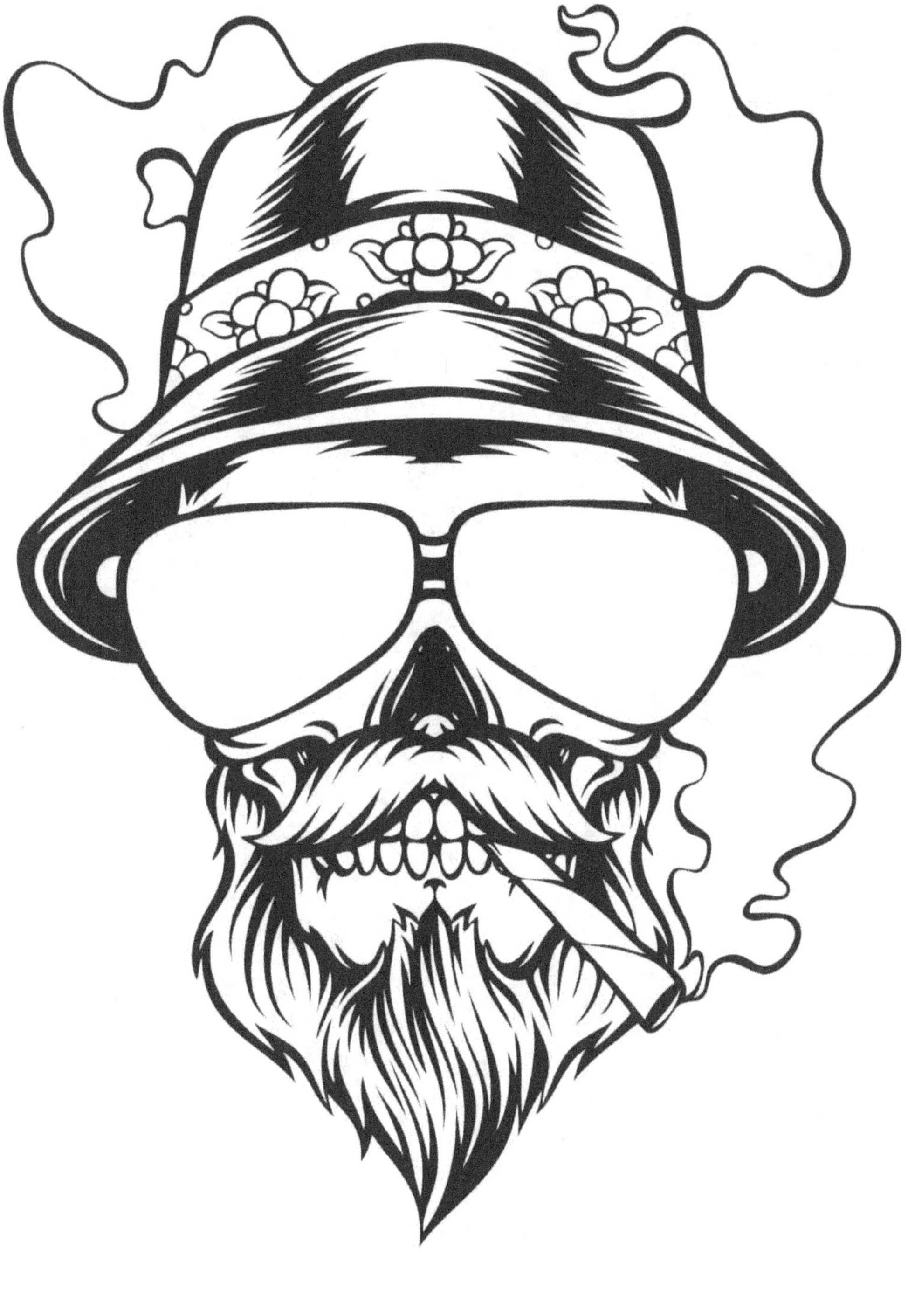

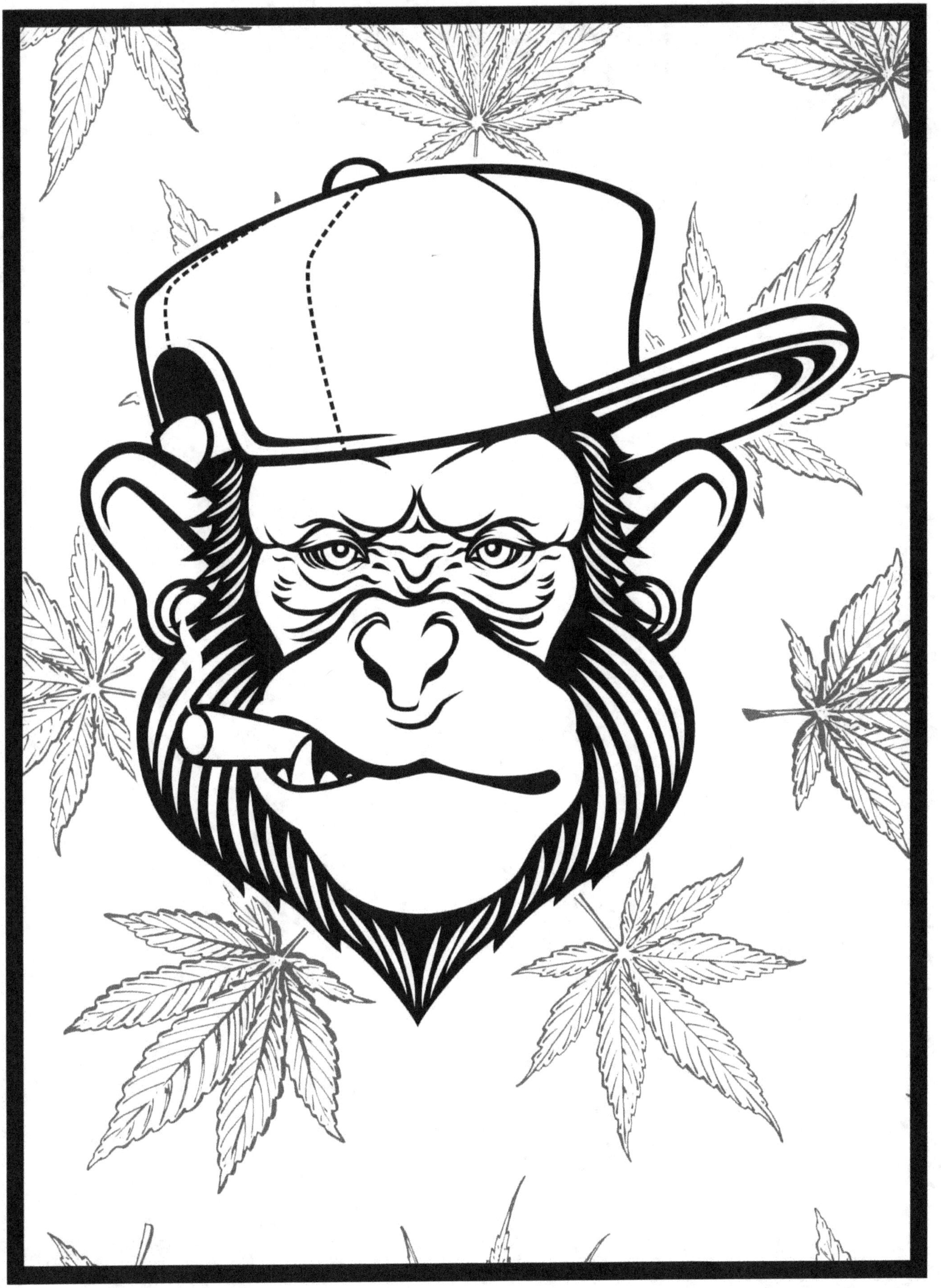

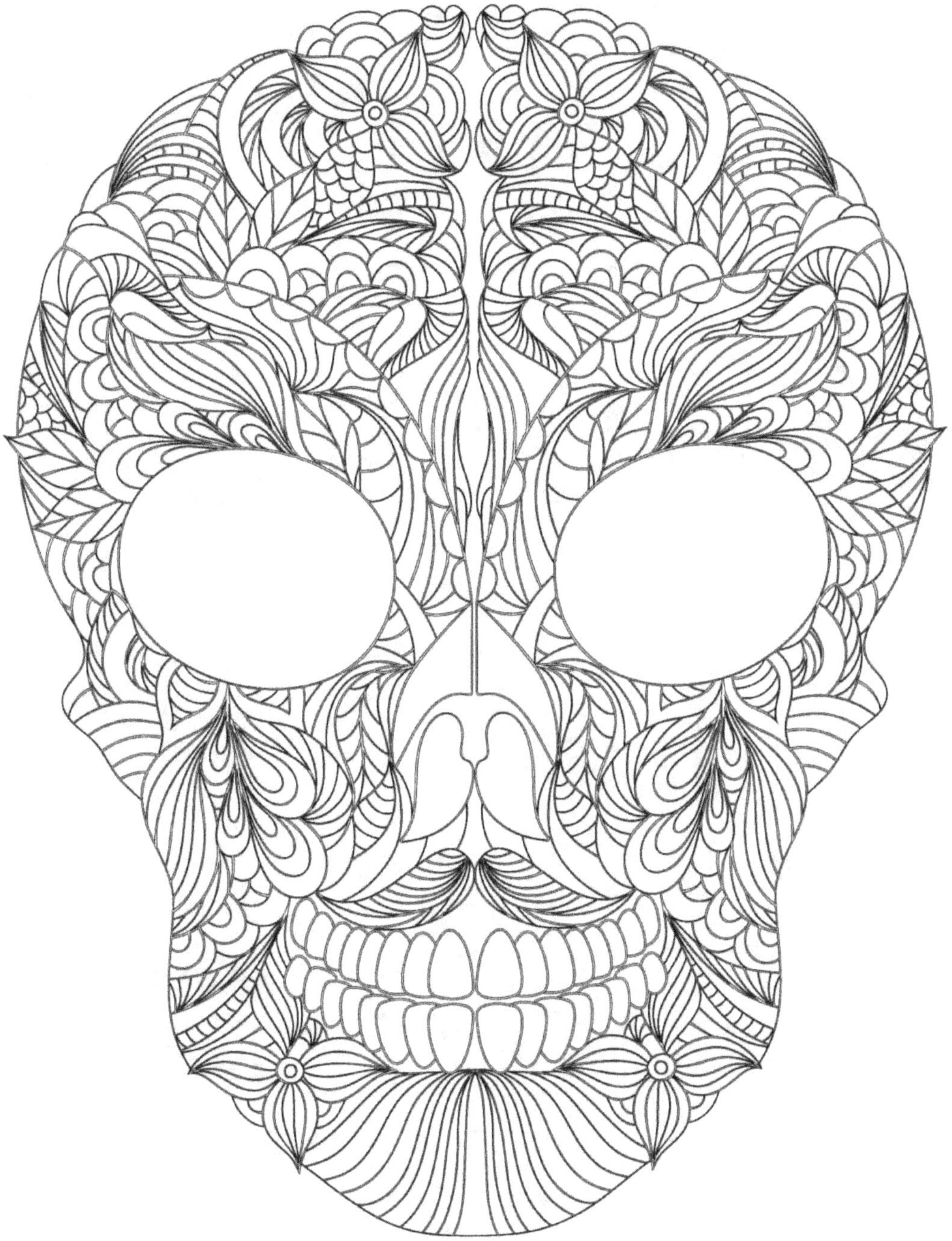

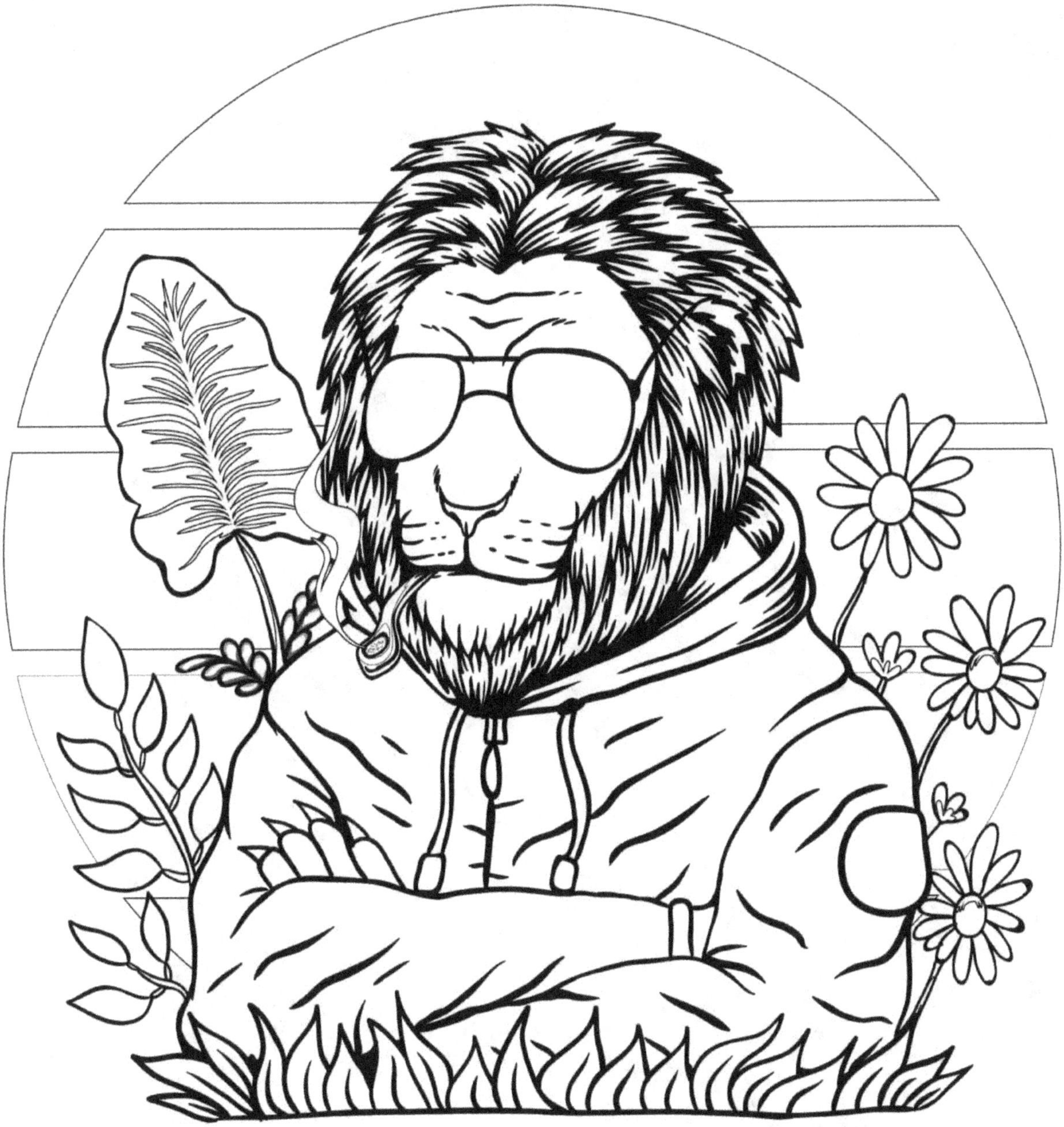

SAVE MY JUNGLE

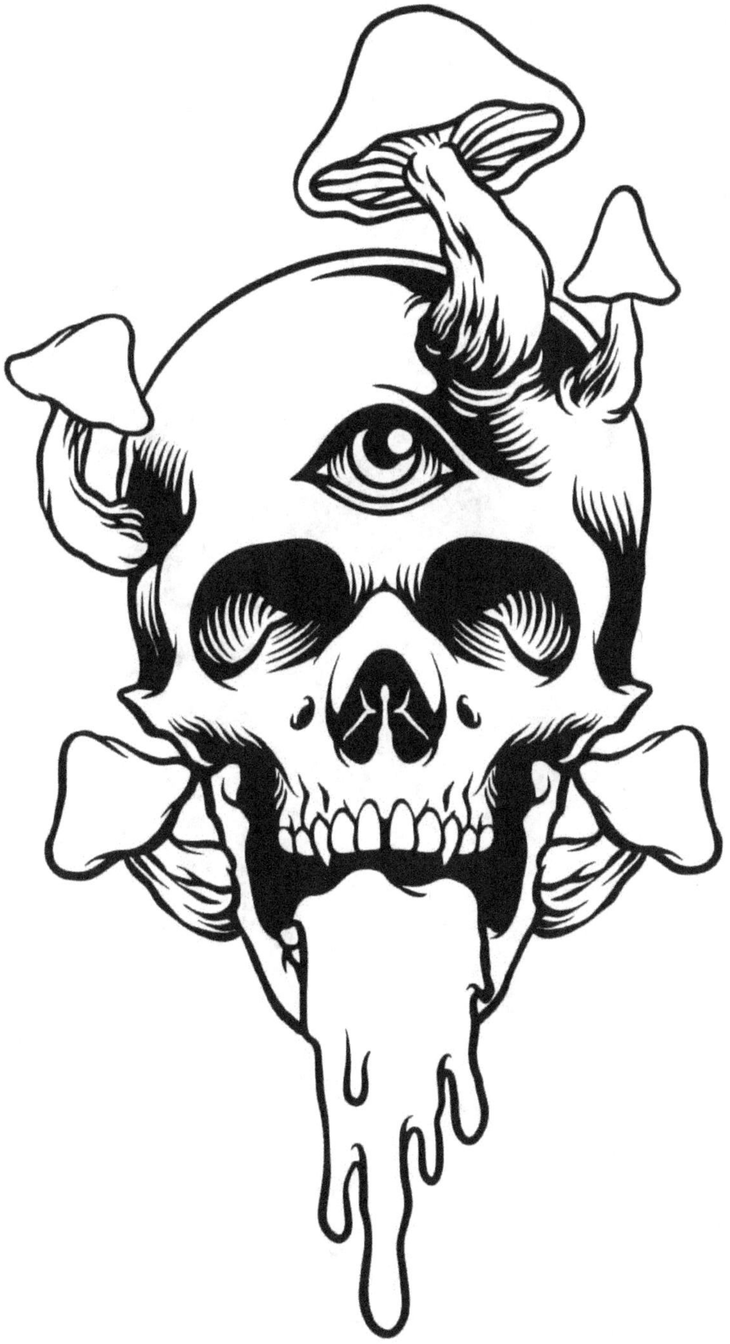

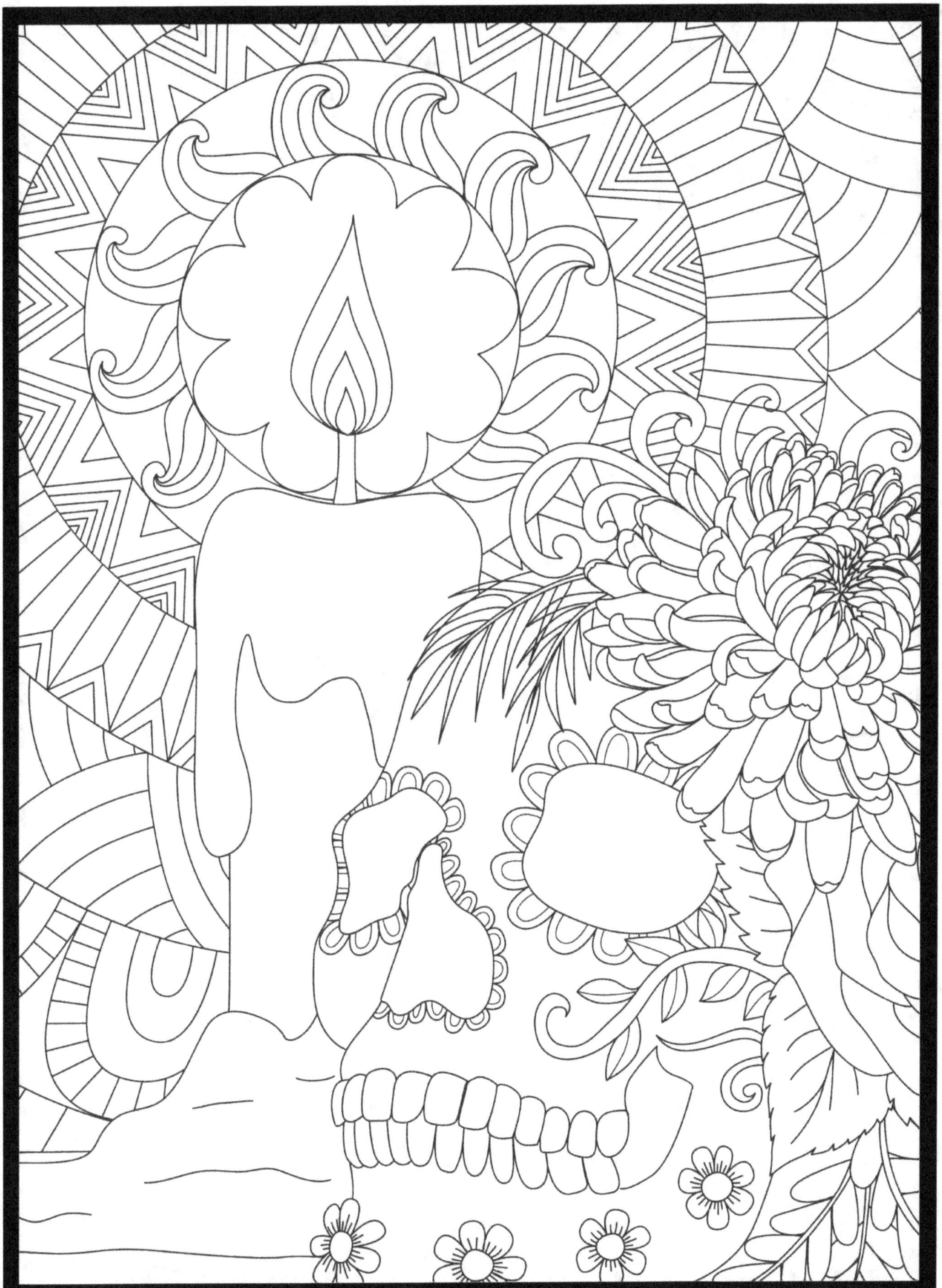

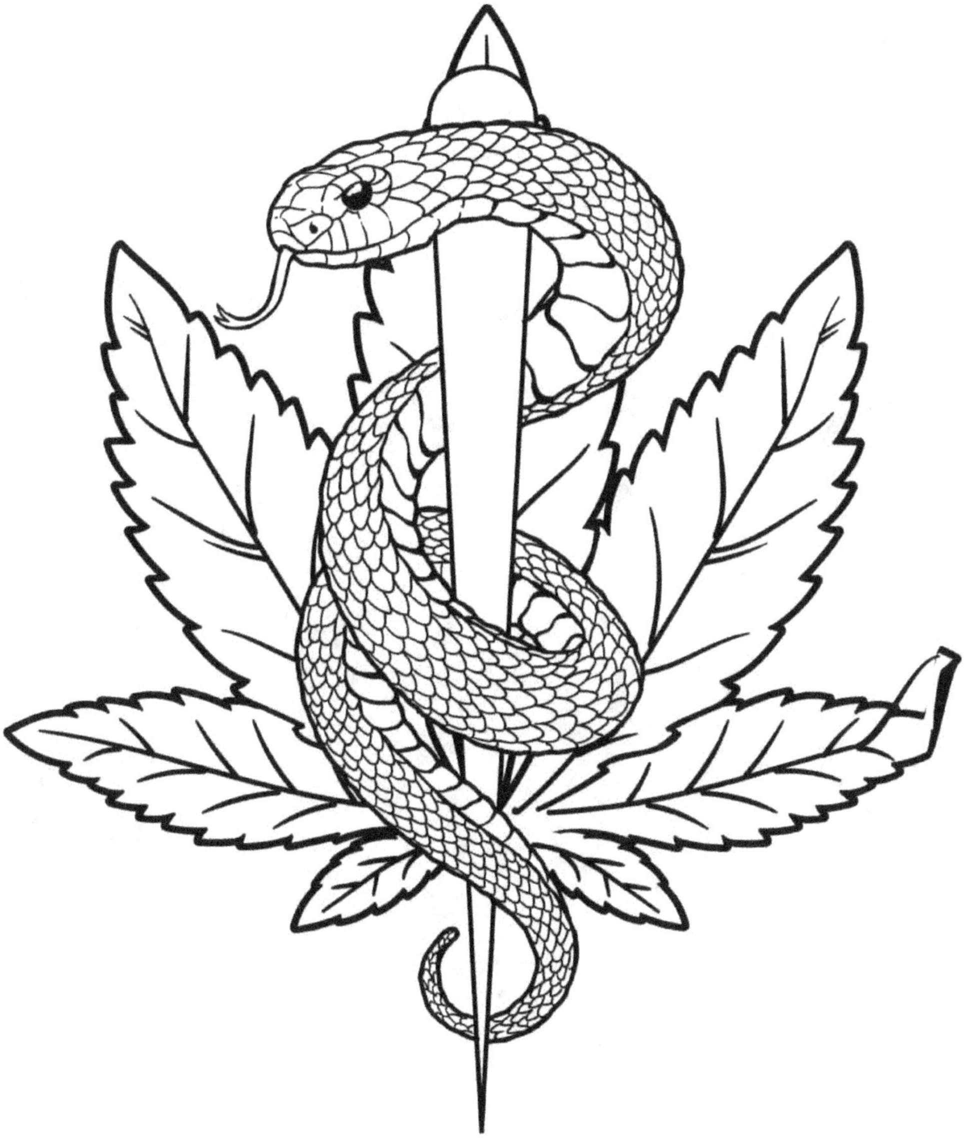

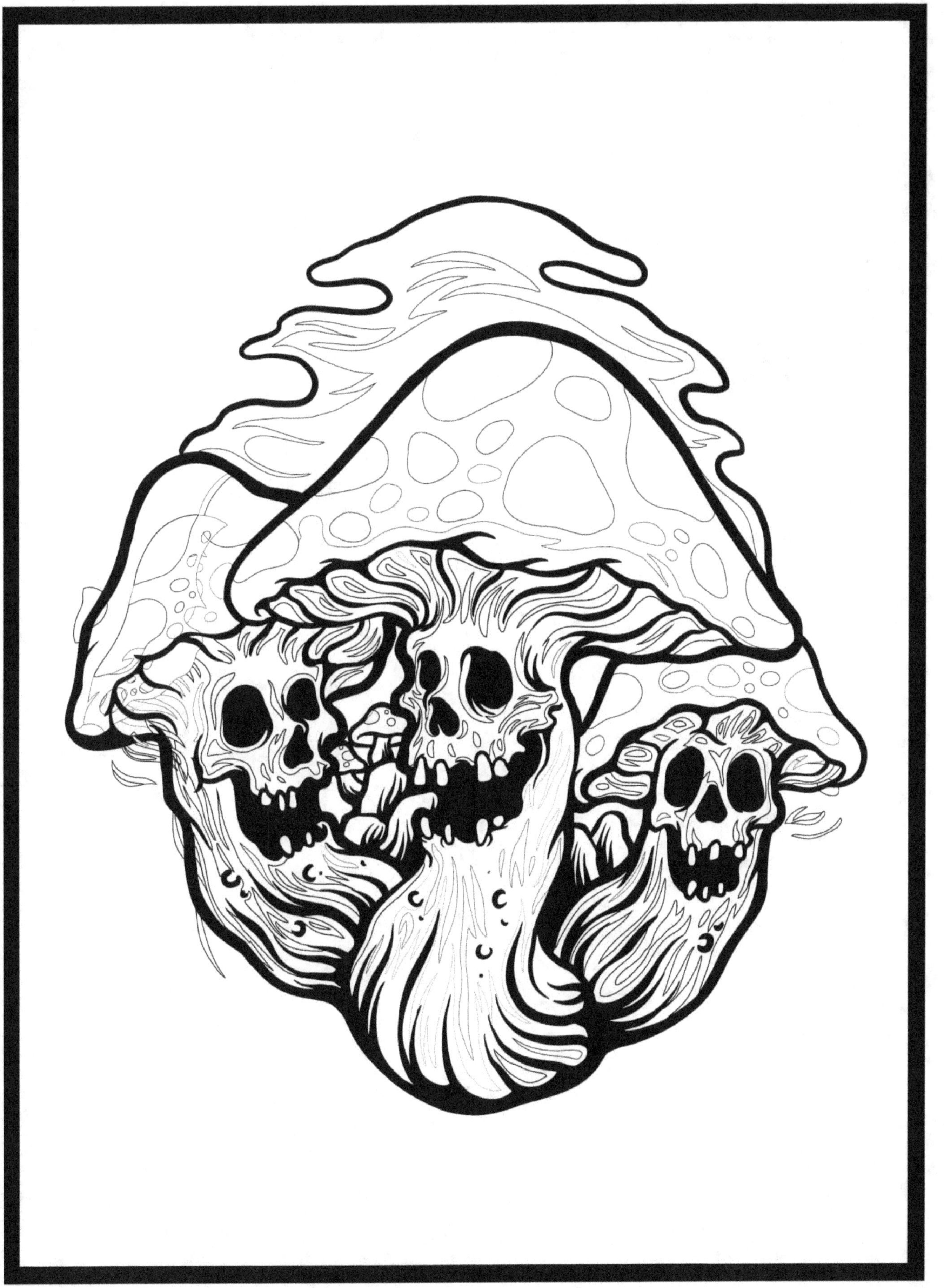

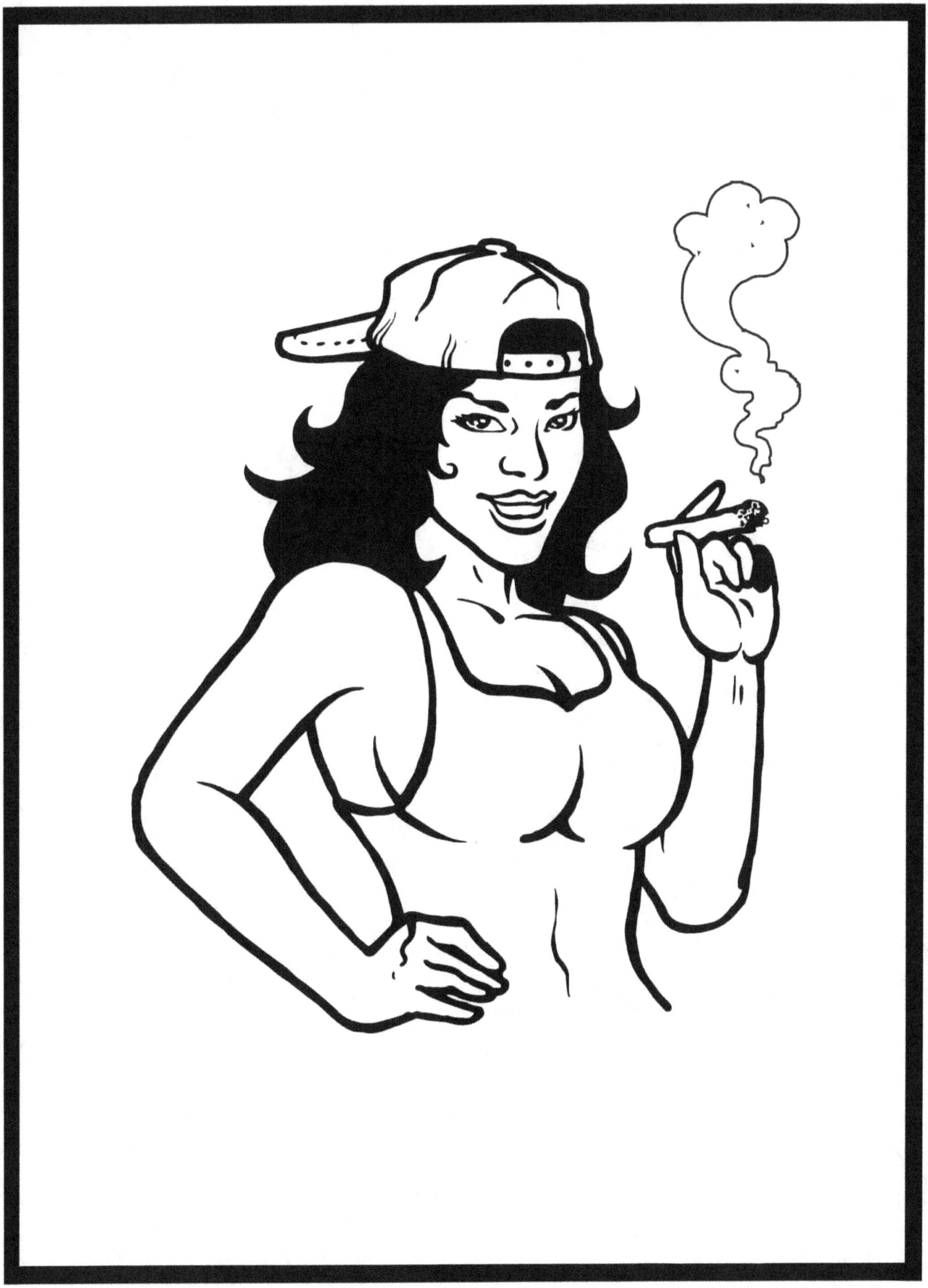

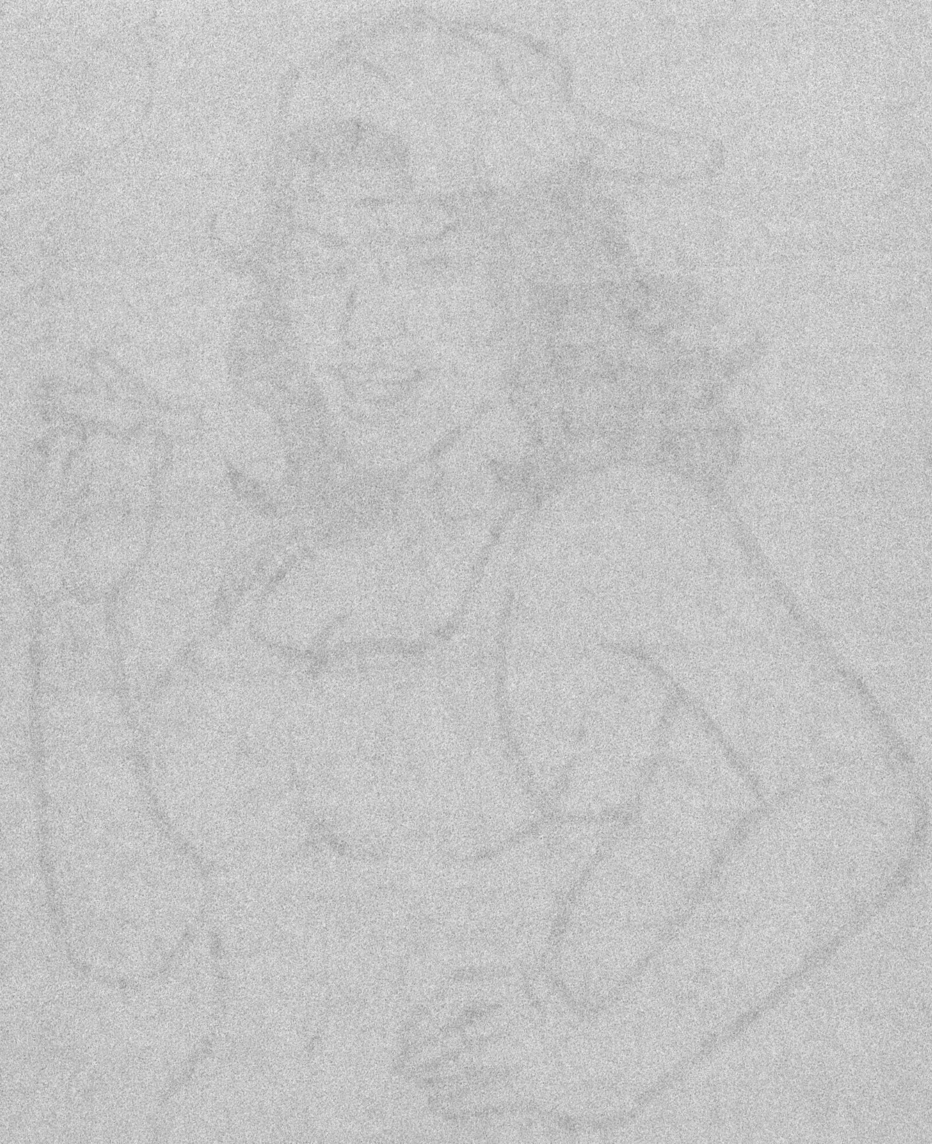

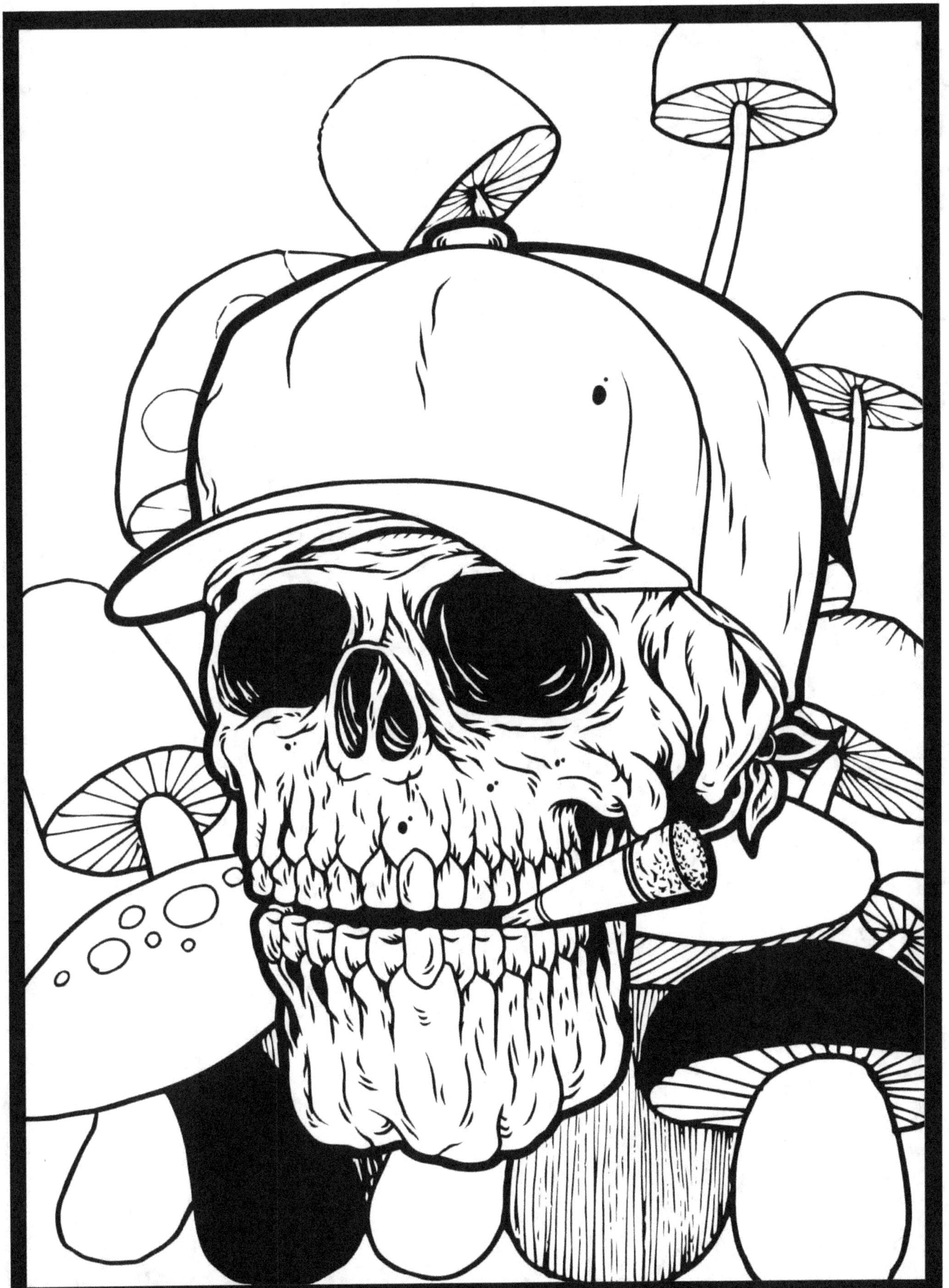

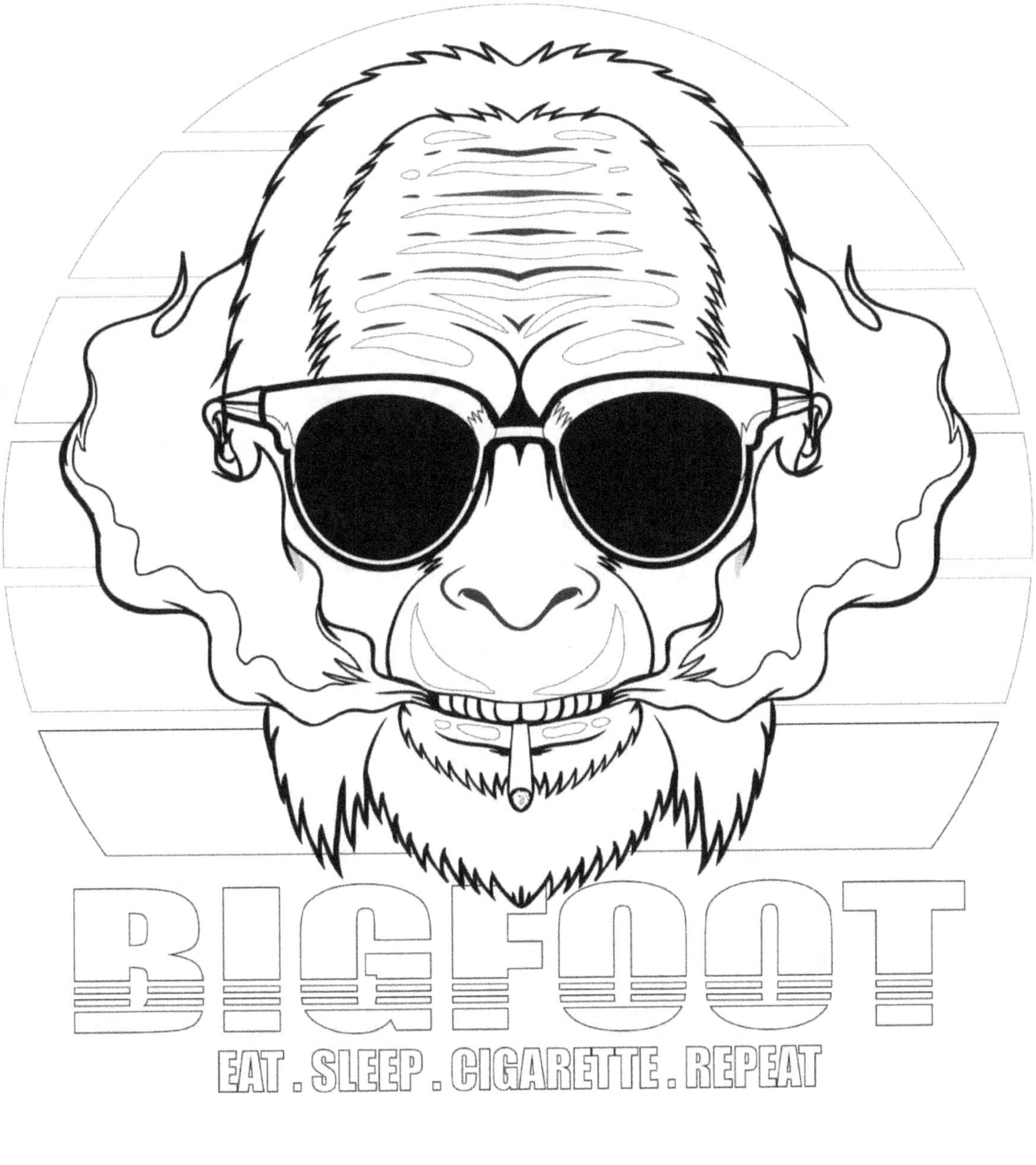
BIGFOOT
EAT . SLEEP . CIGARETTE . REPEAT

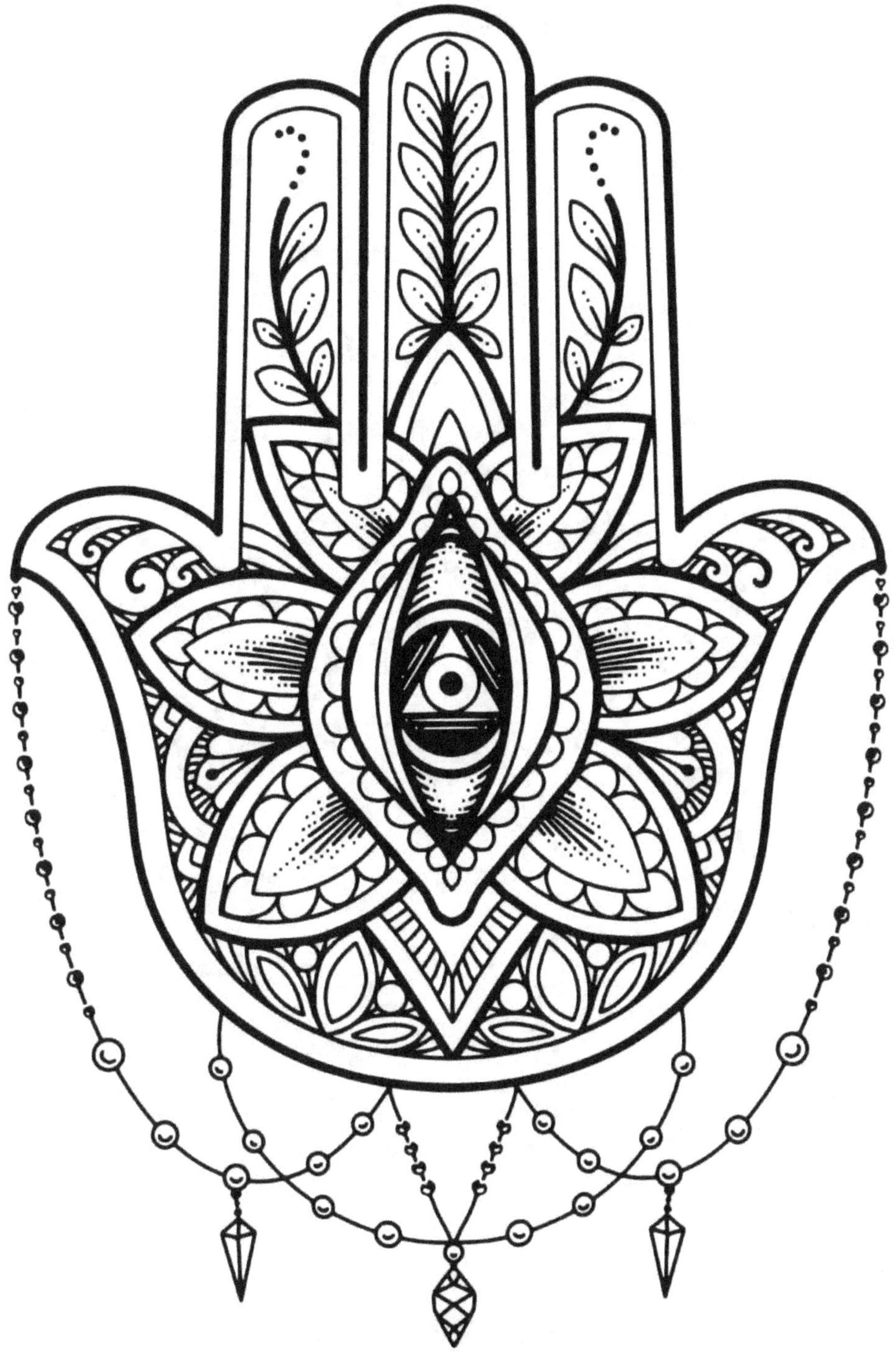

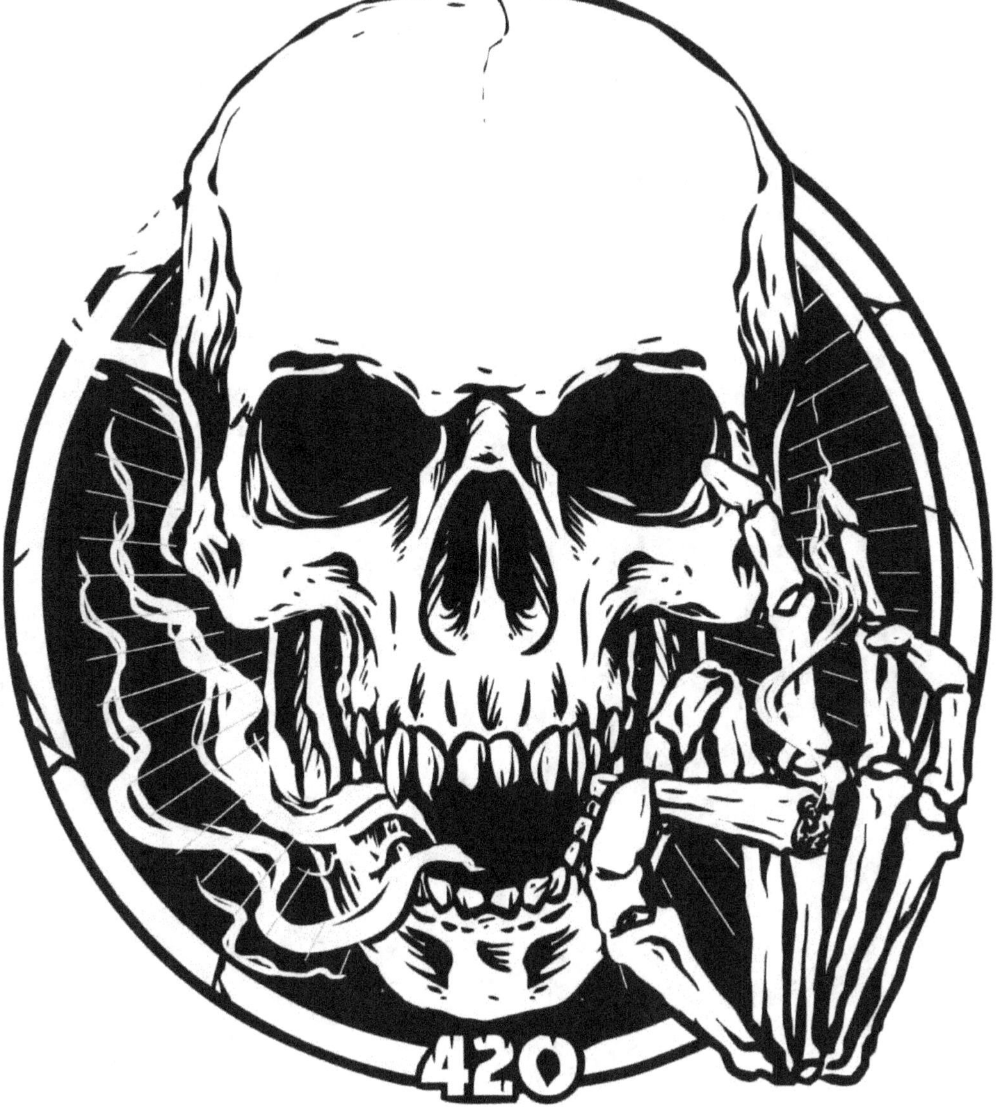
420

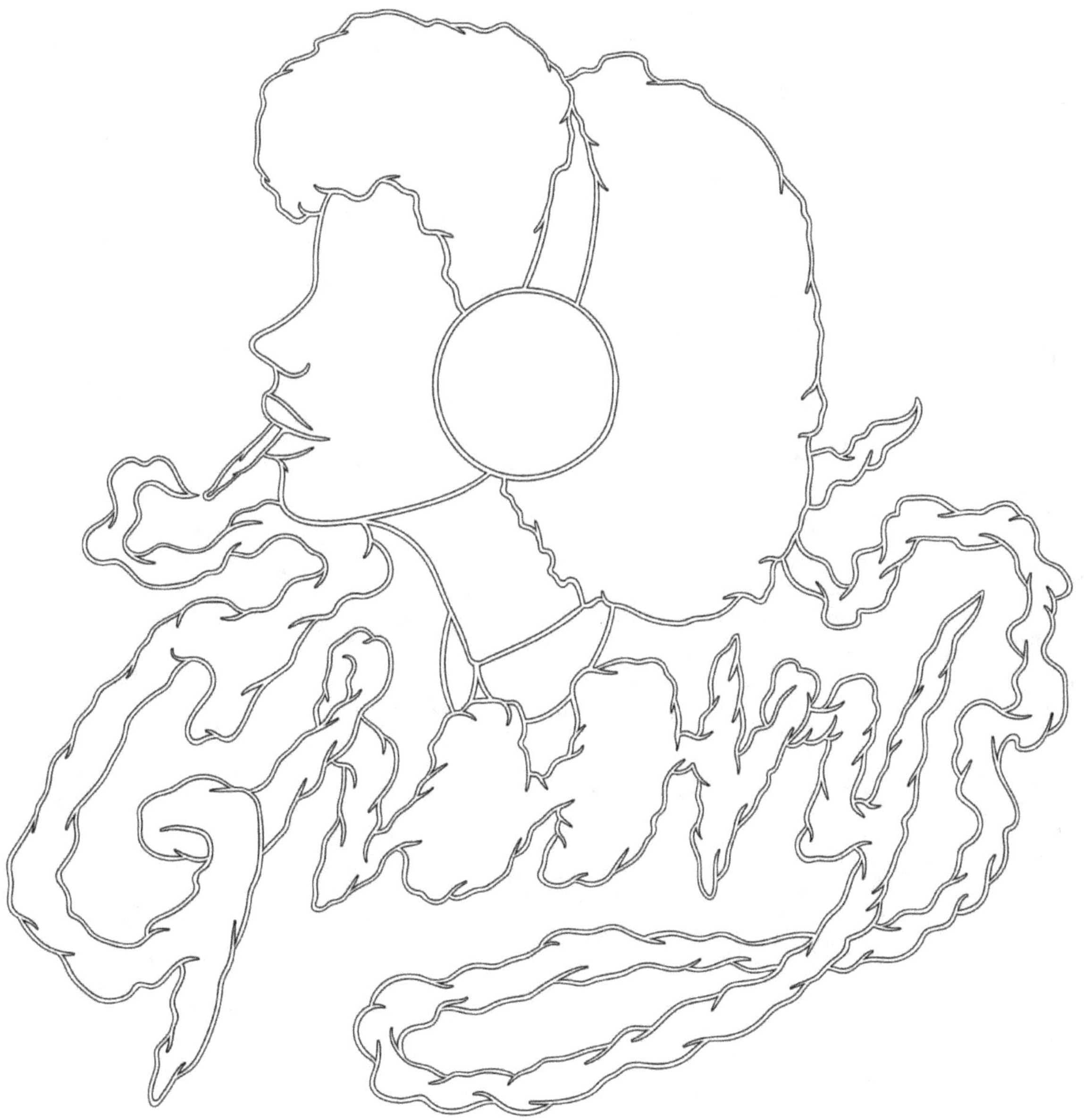

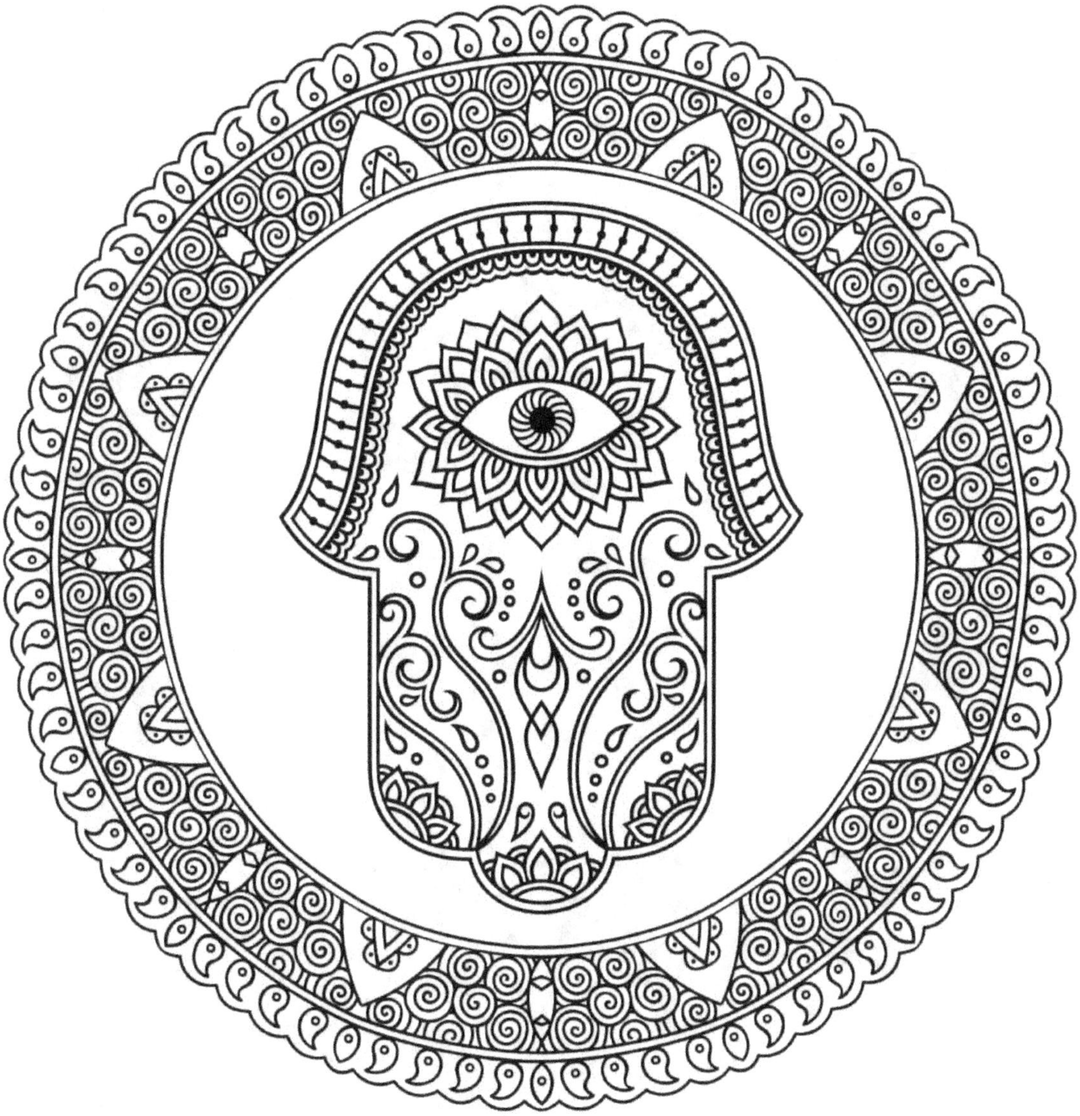

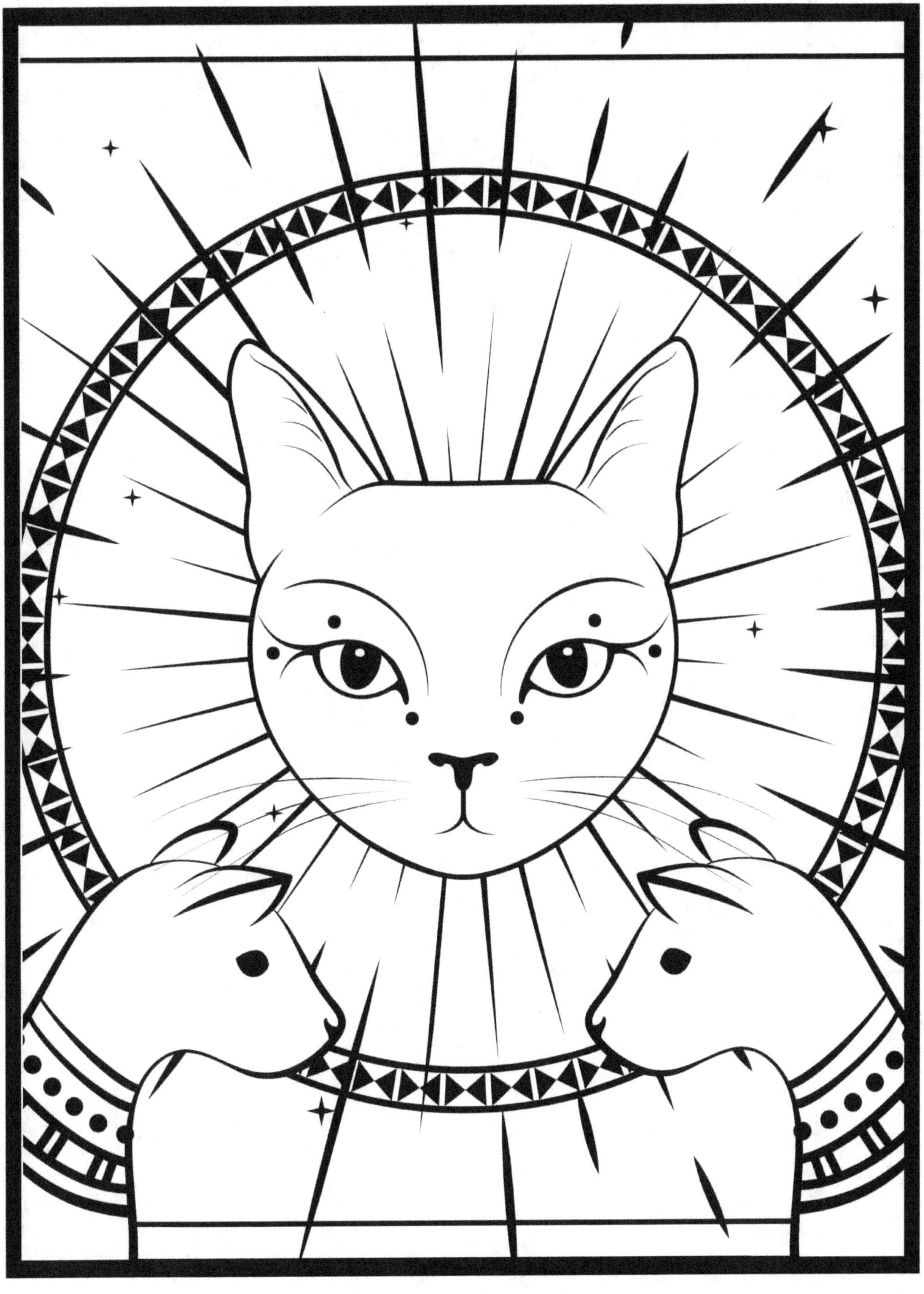

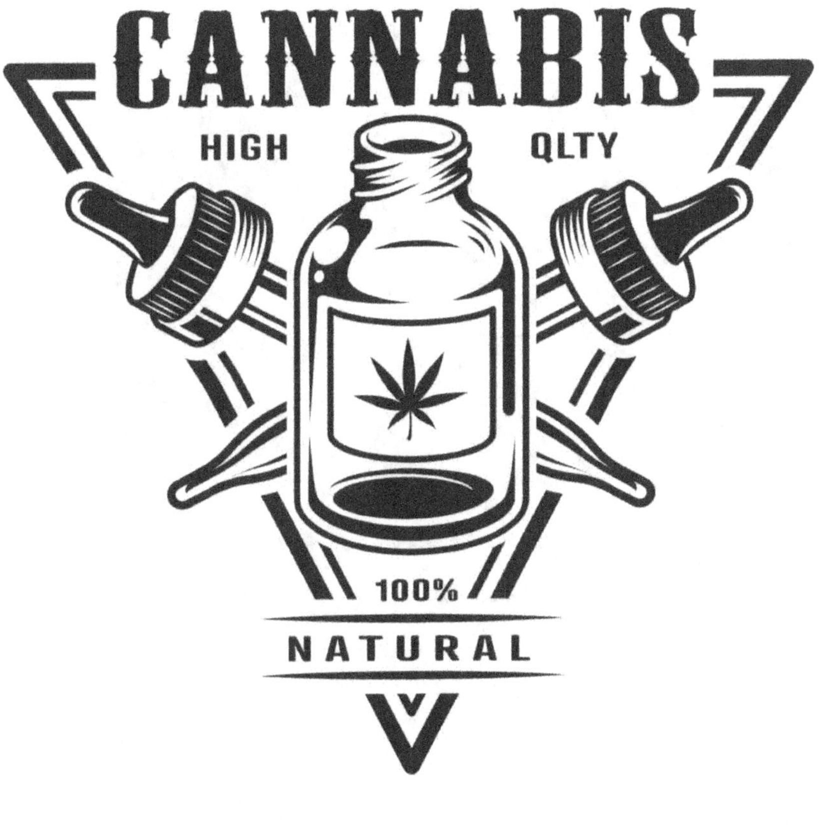
CANNABIS
HIGH
QLTY
100%
NATURAL

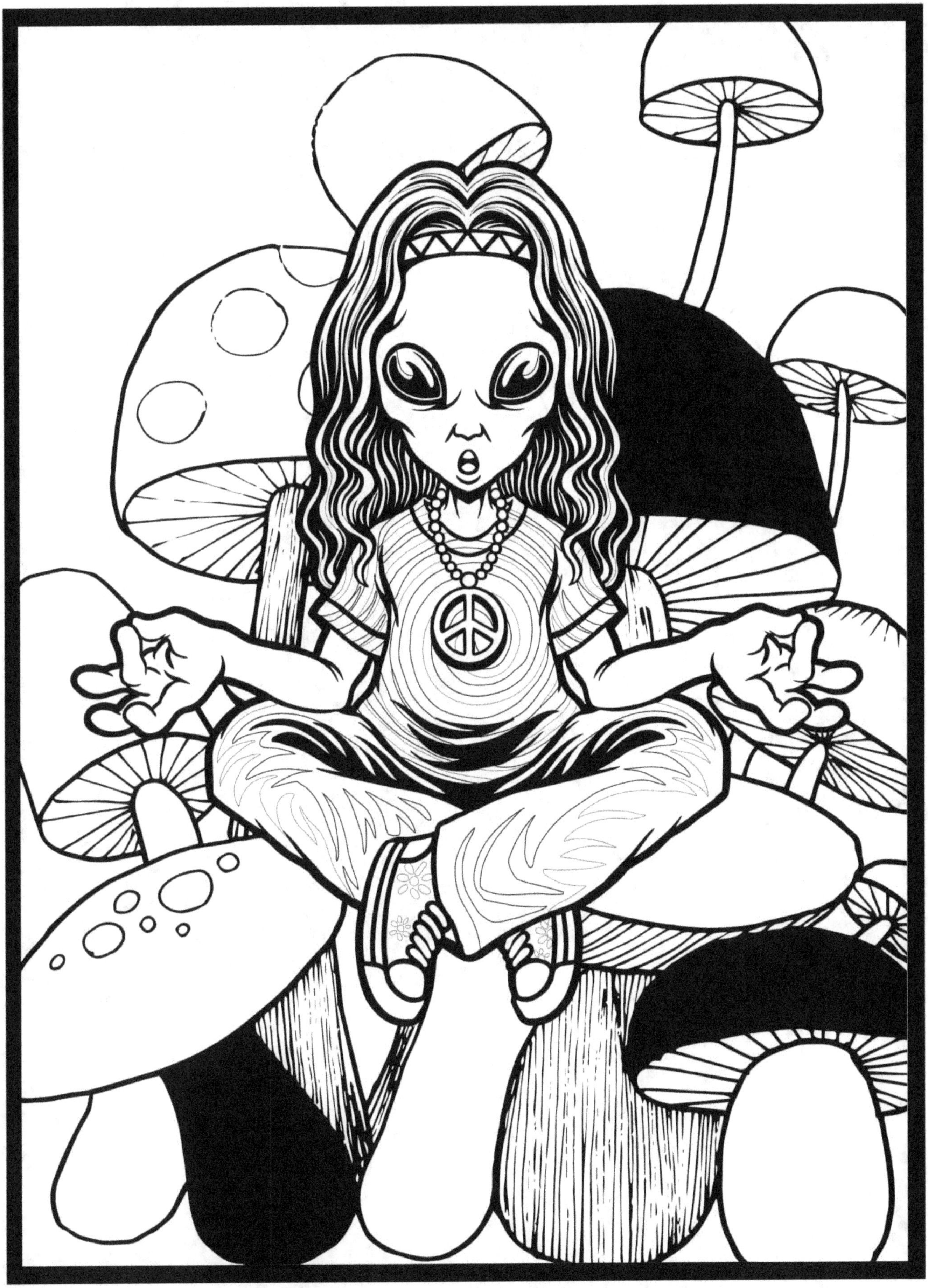

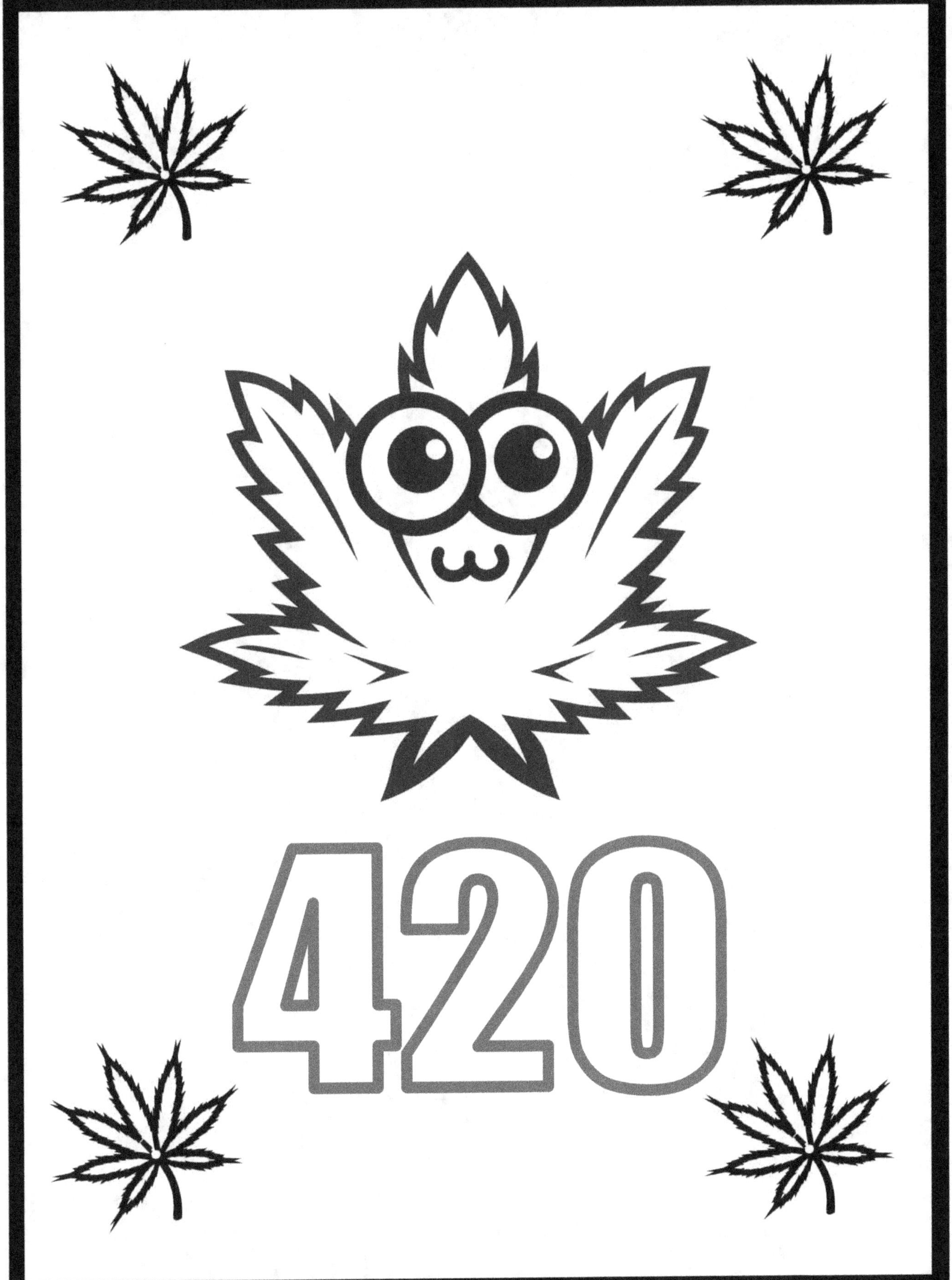
420

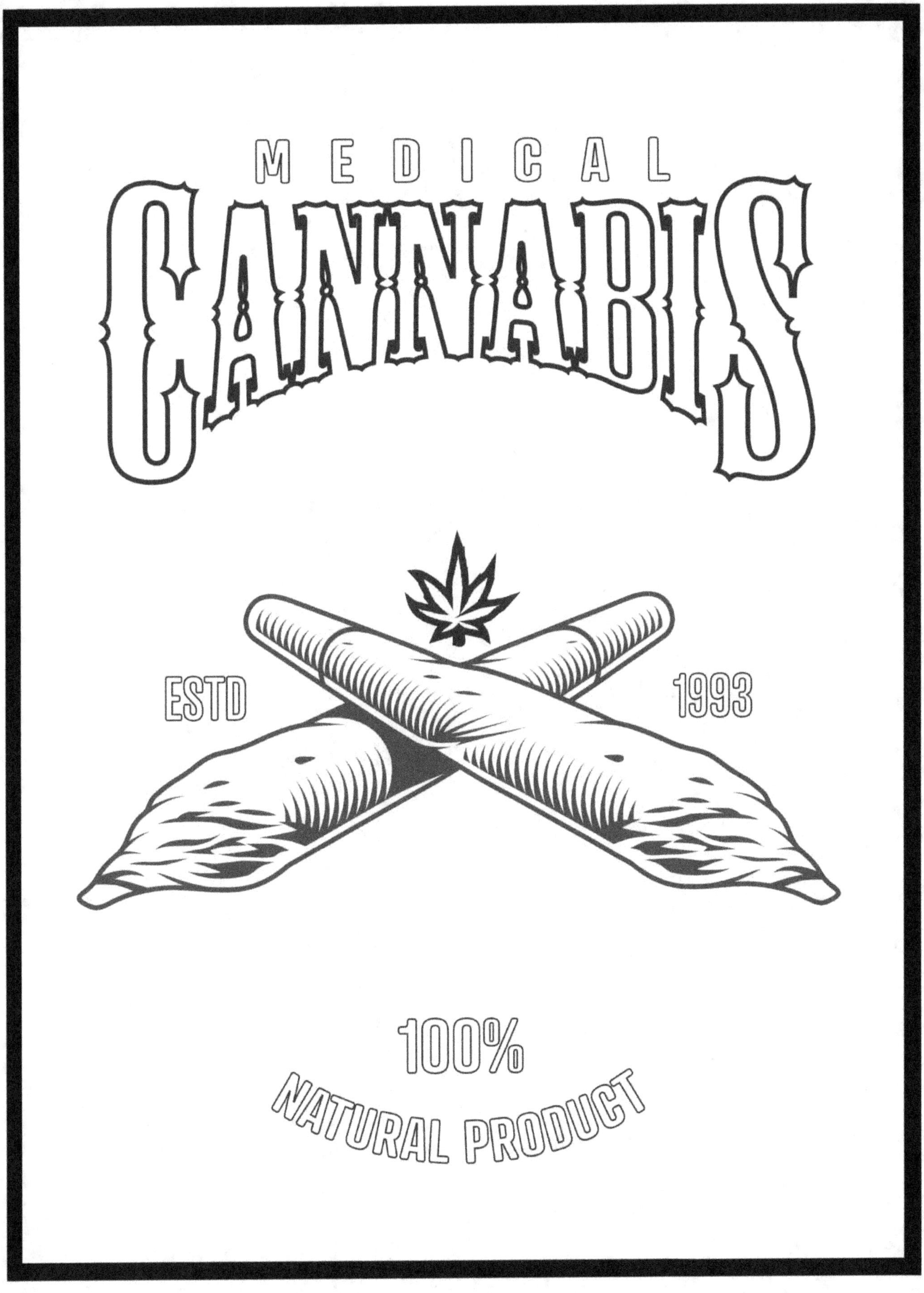
MEDICAL
CANNABIS
ESTD
1993
100%
NATURAL PRODUCT

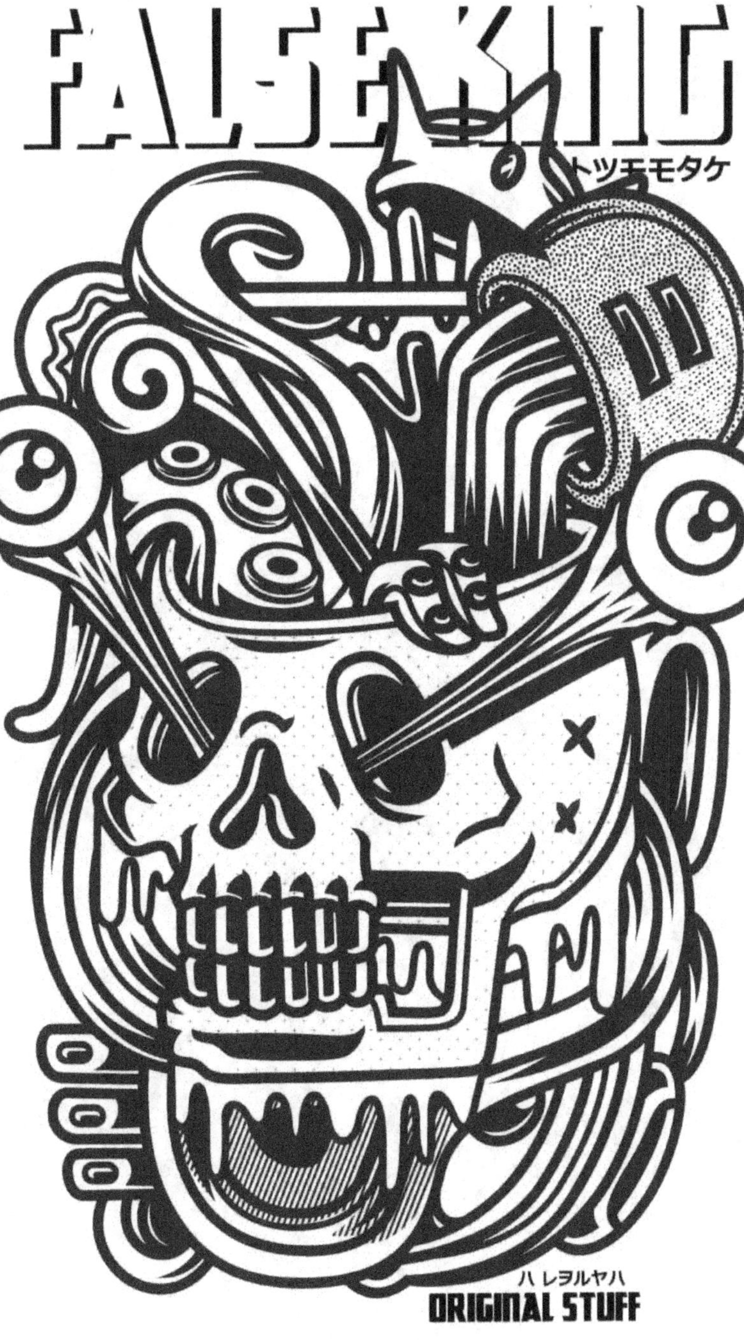
FALSE KING
トツモモタケ
ハ レヲルヤハ
ORIGINAL STUFF

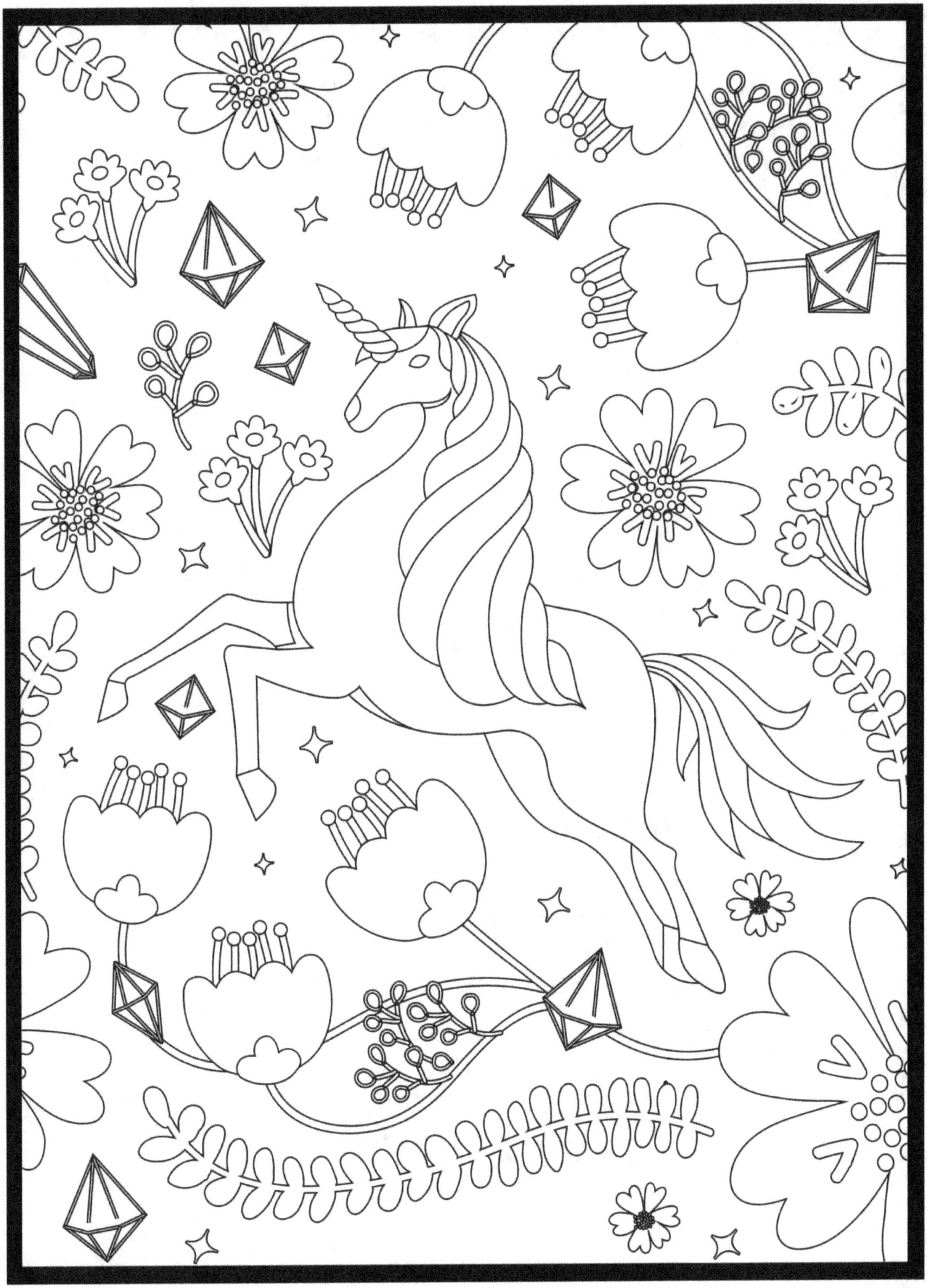

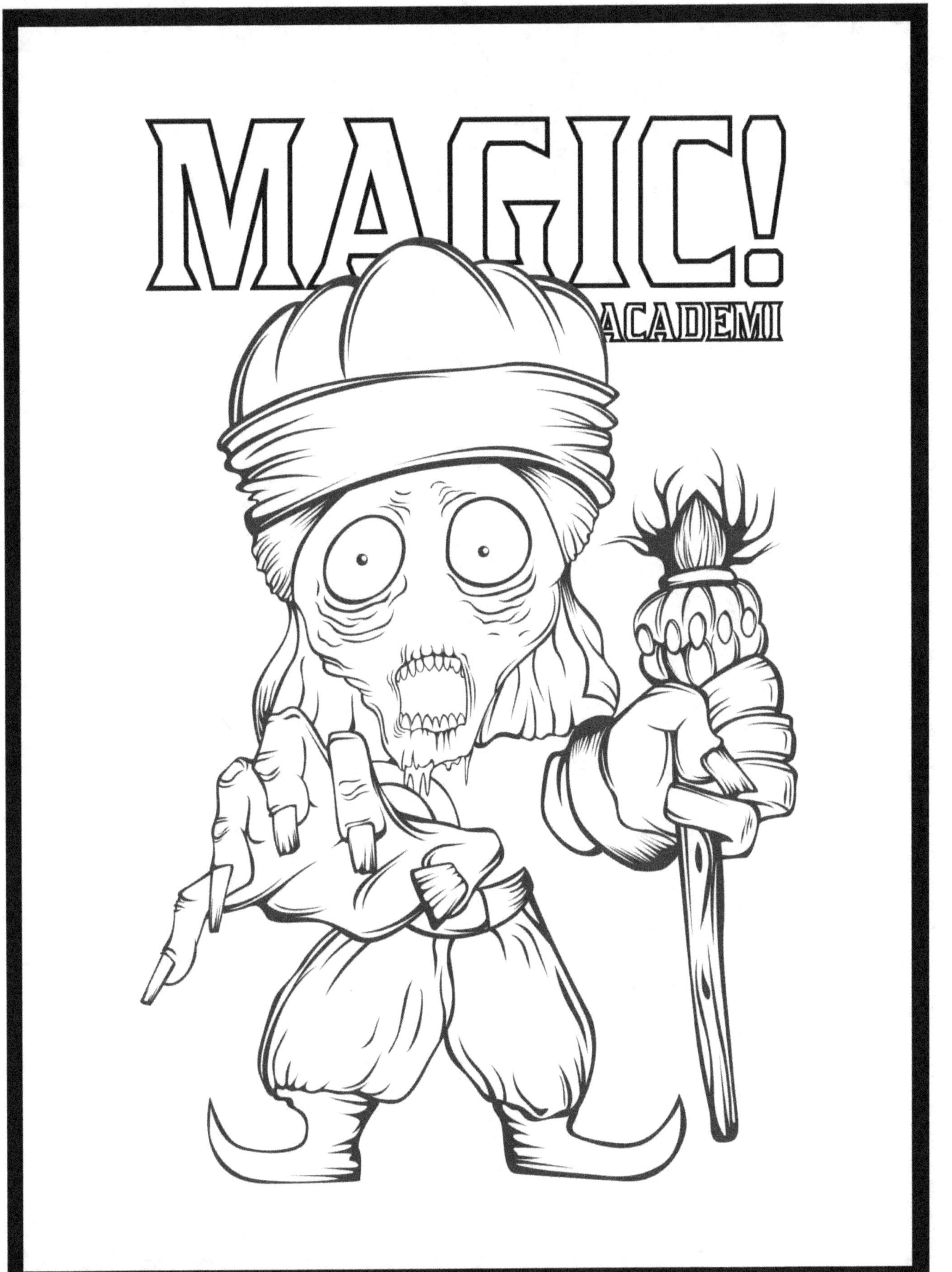
MAGIC!
ACADEMI

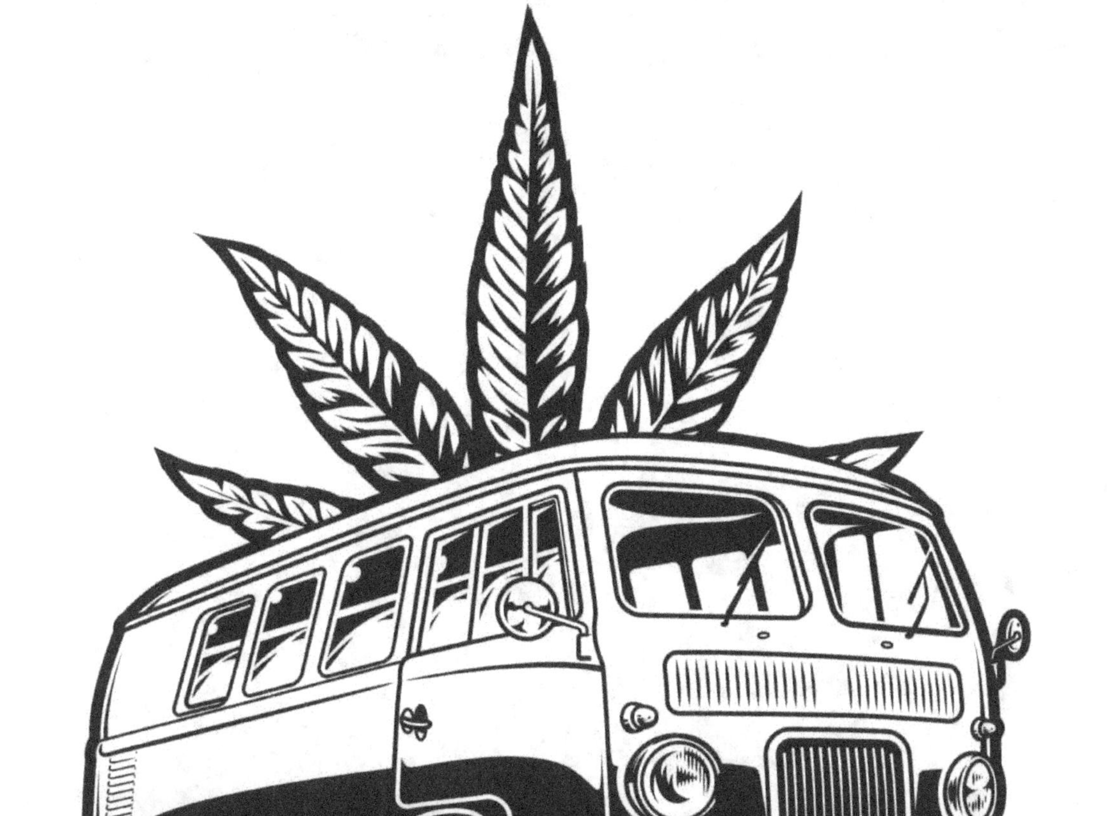
FREEDOM
CLUB

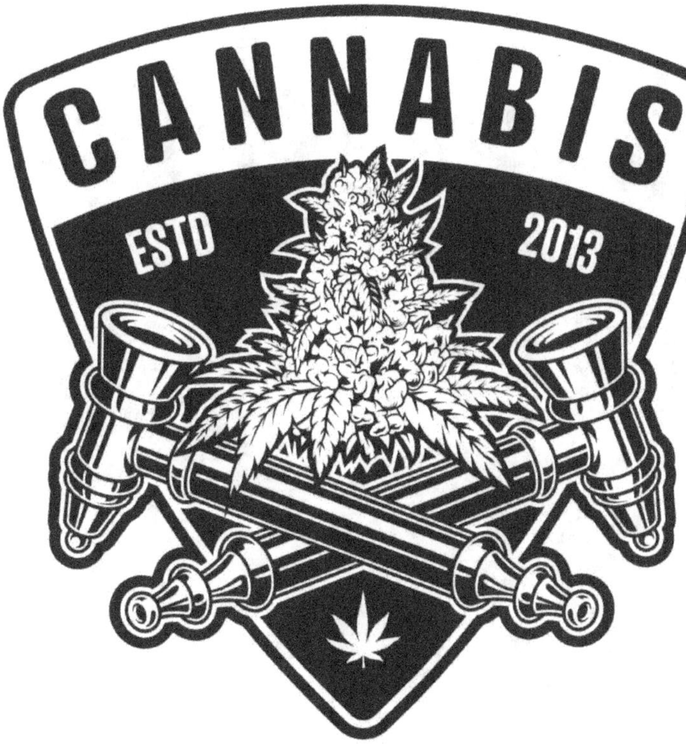
CANNABIS
ESTD
2013

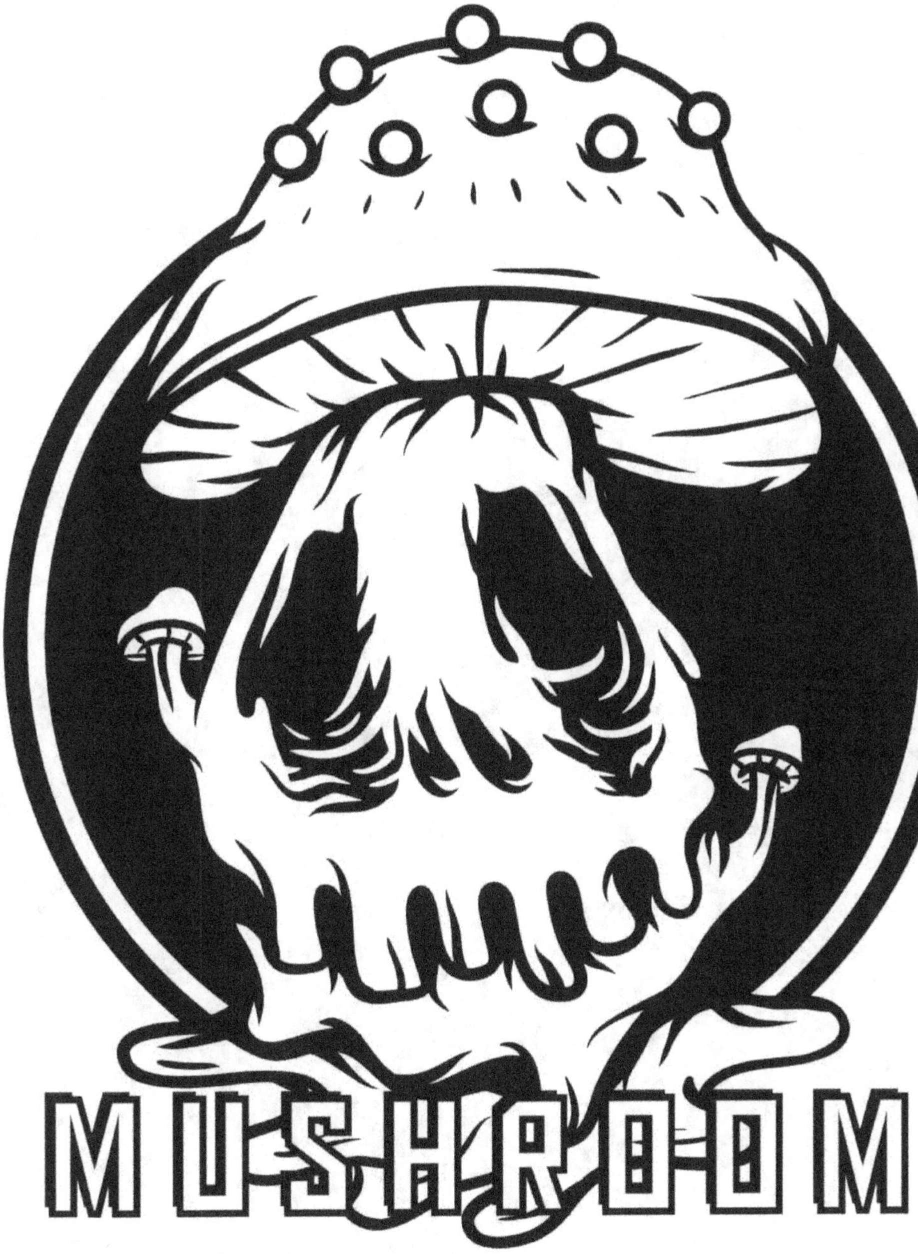
MUSHROOM

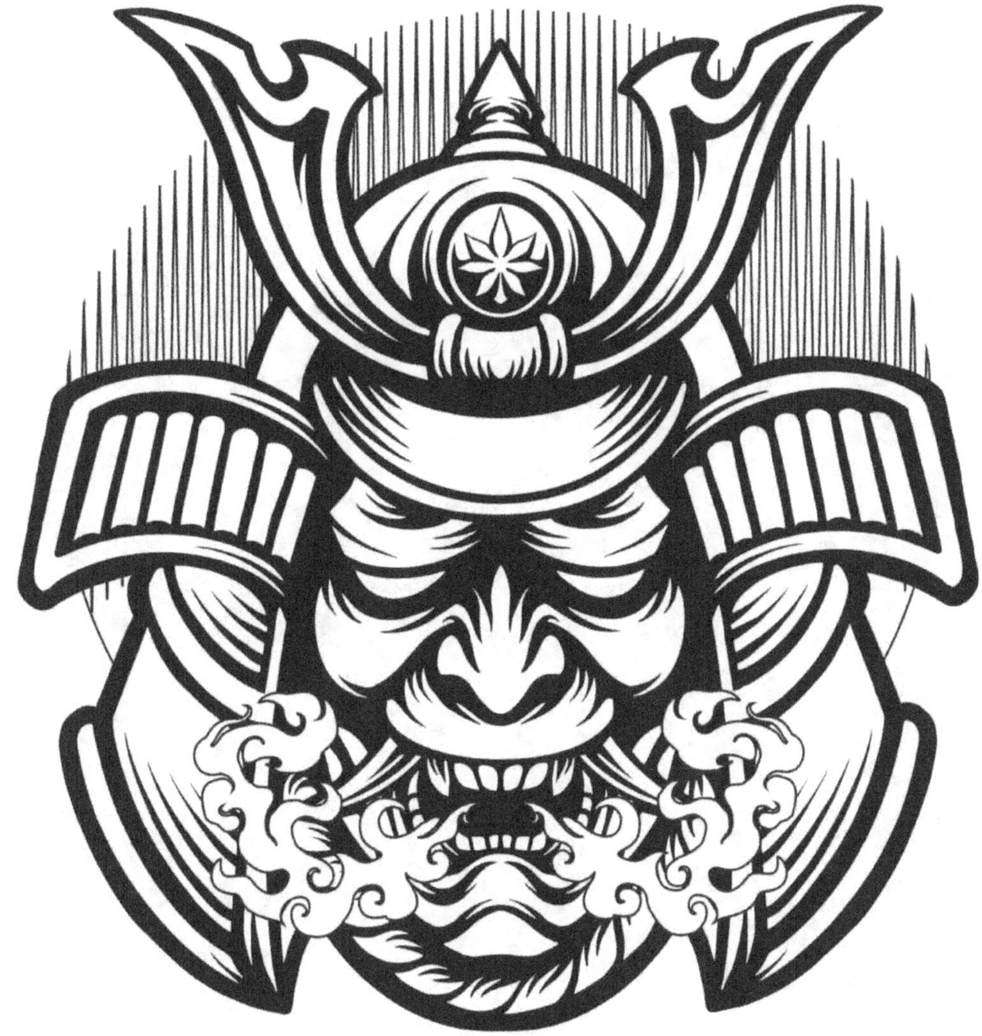

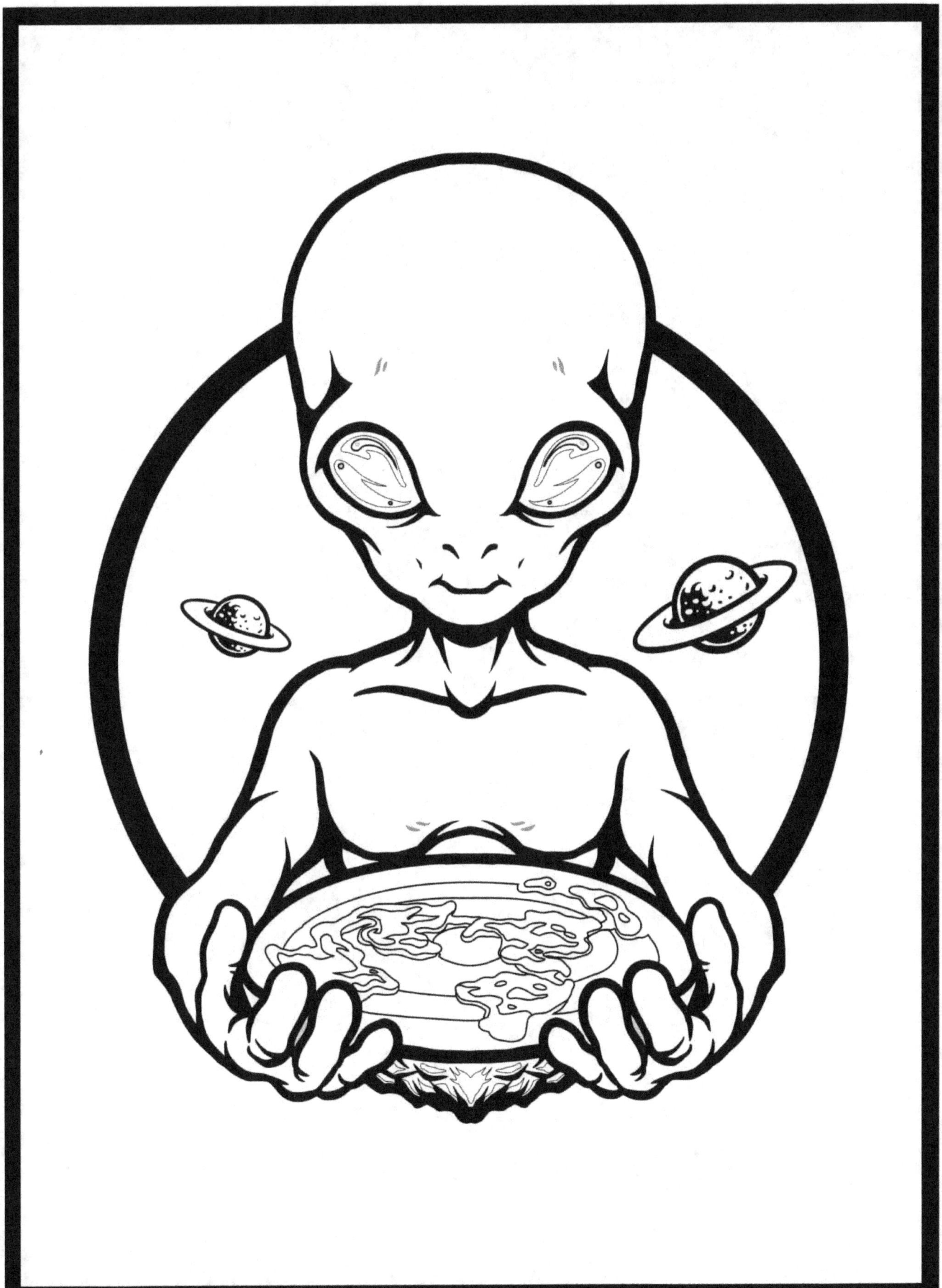

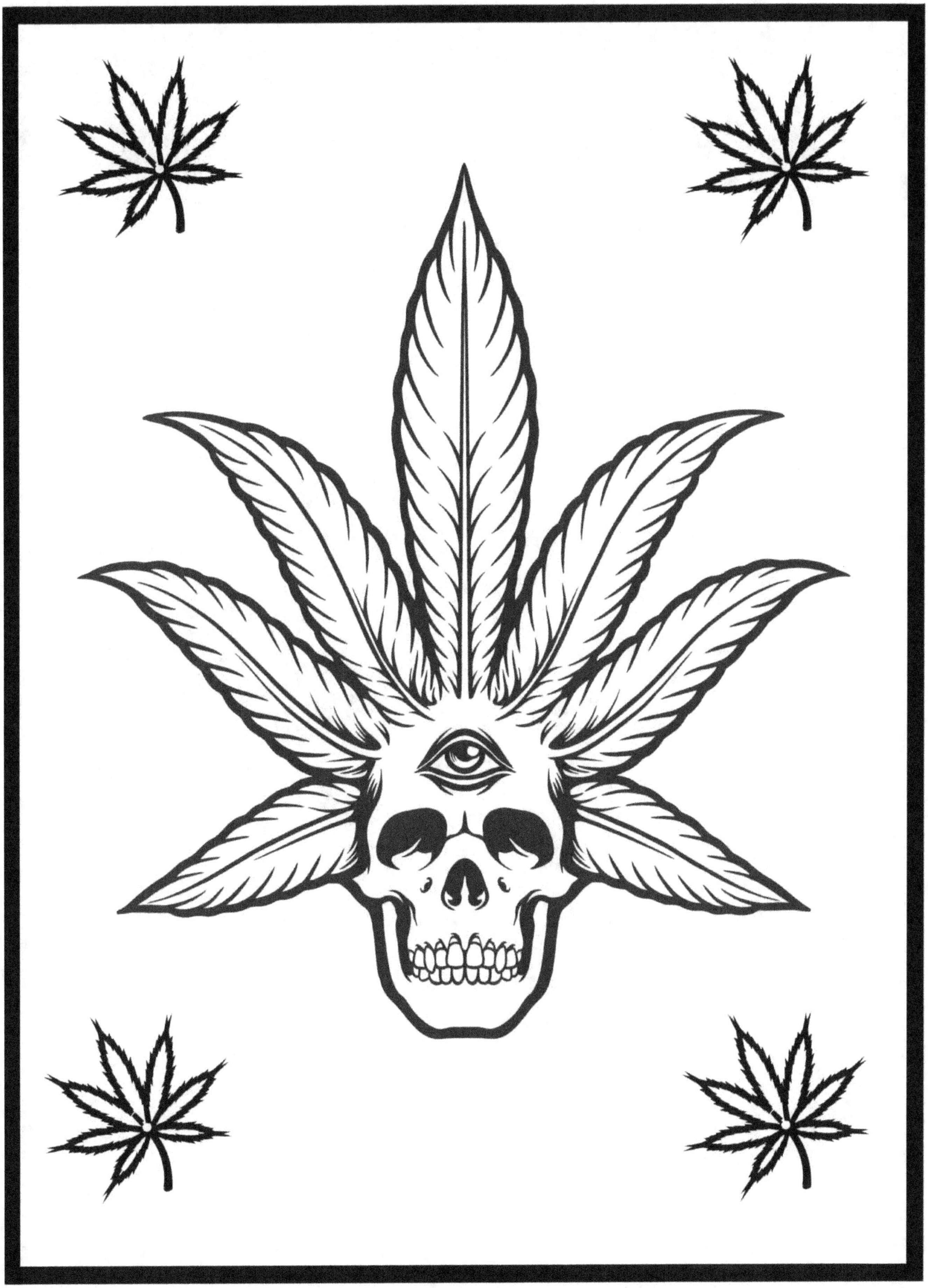

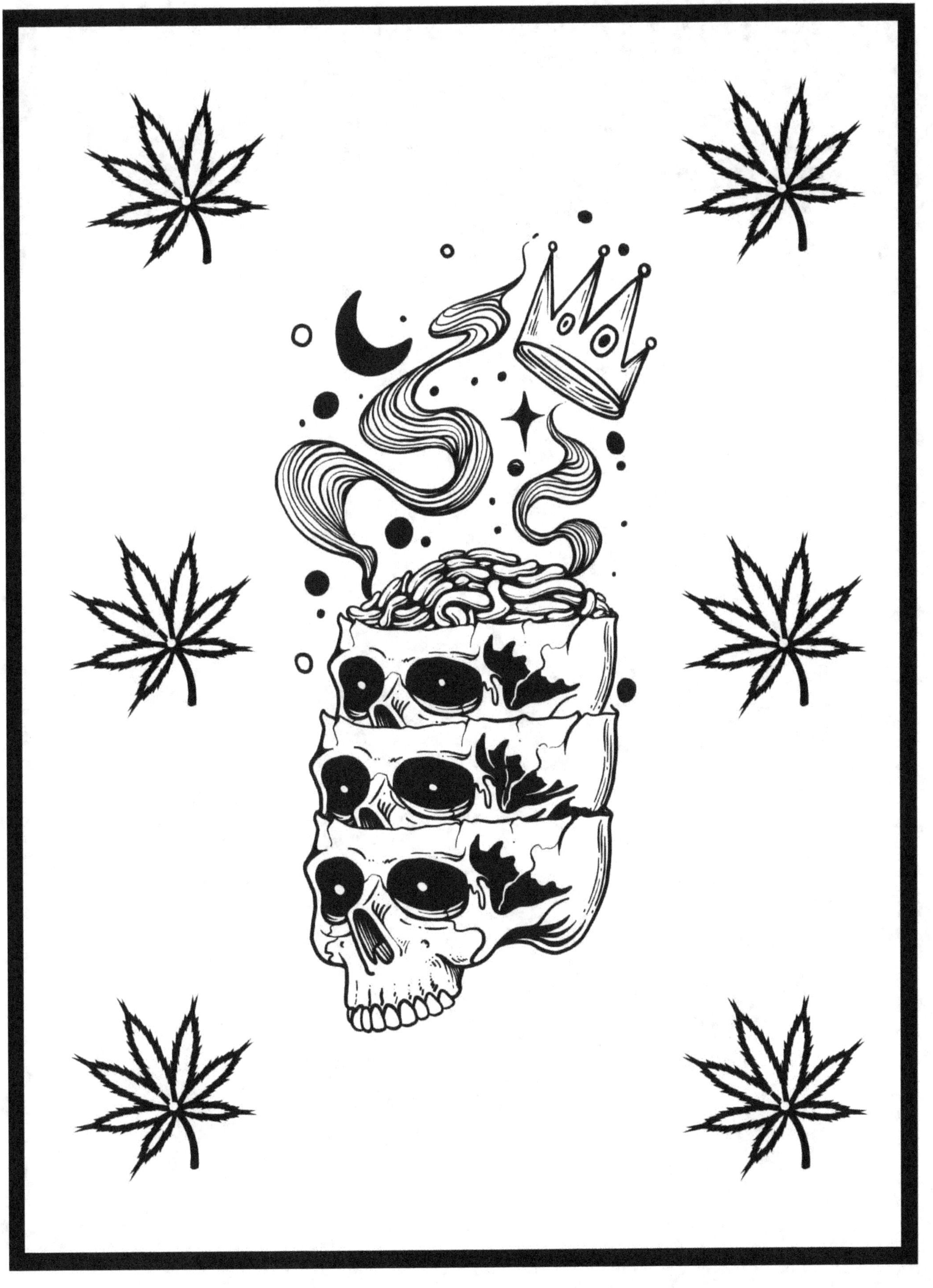

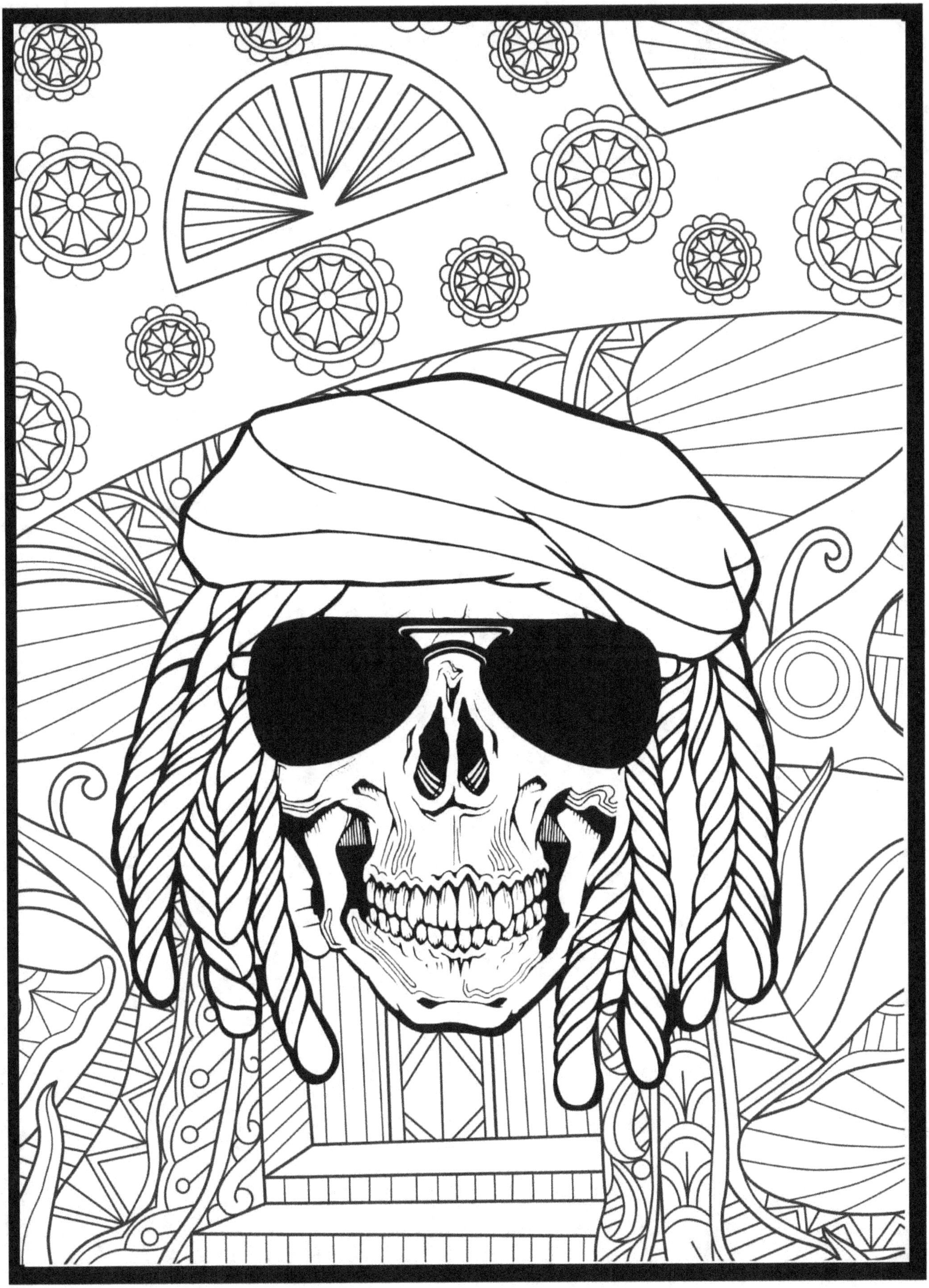

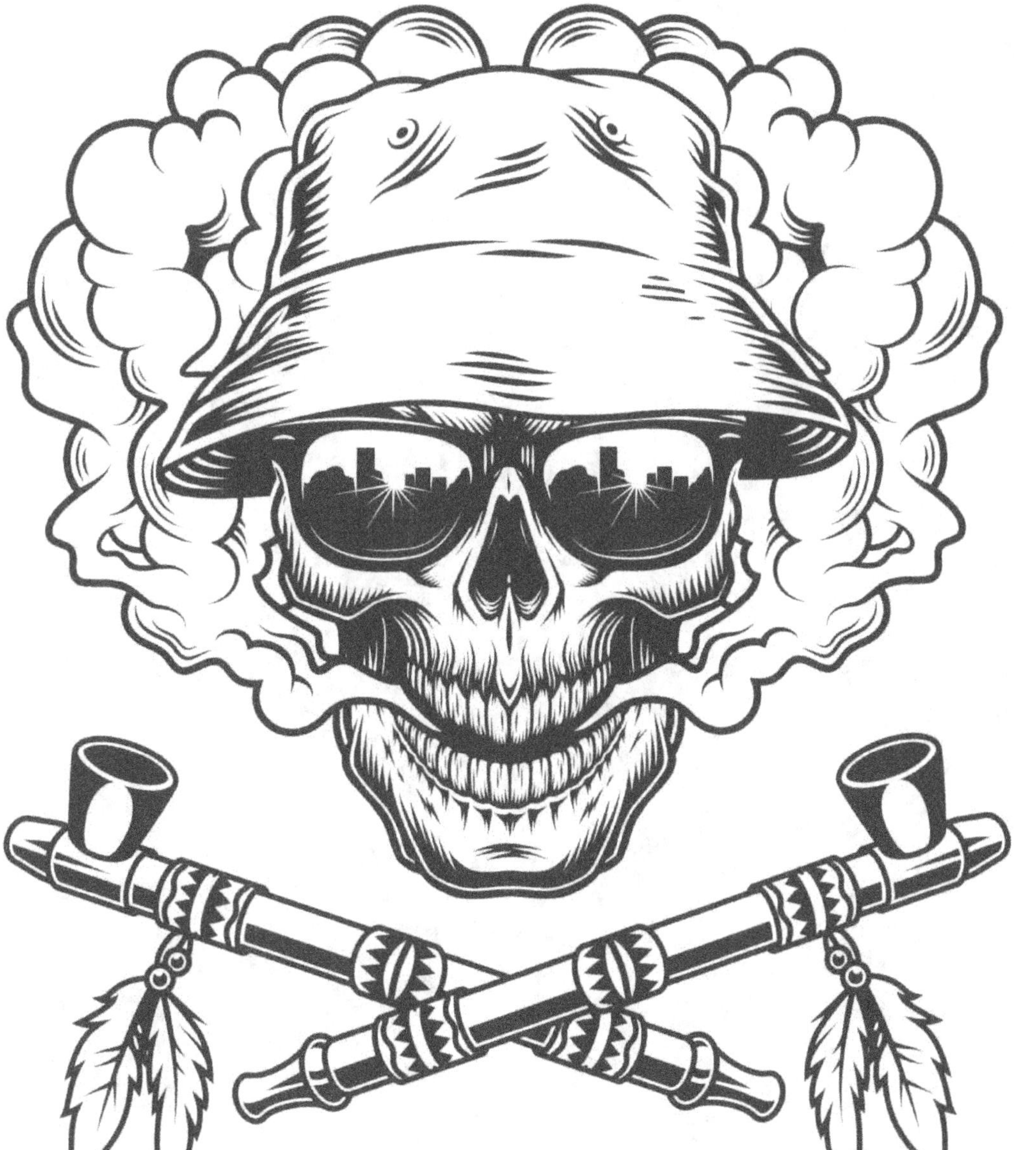

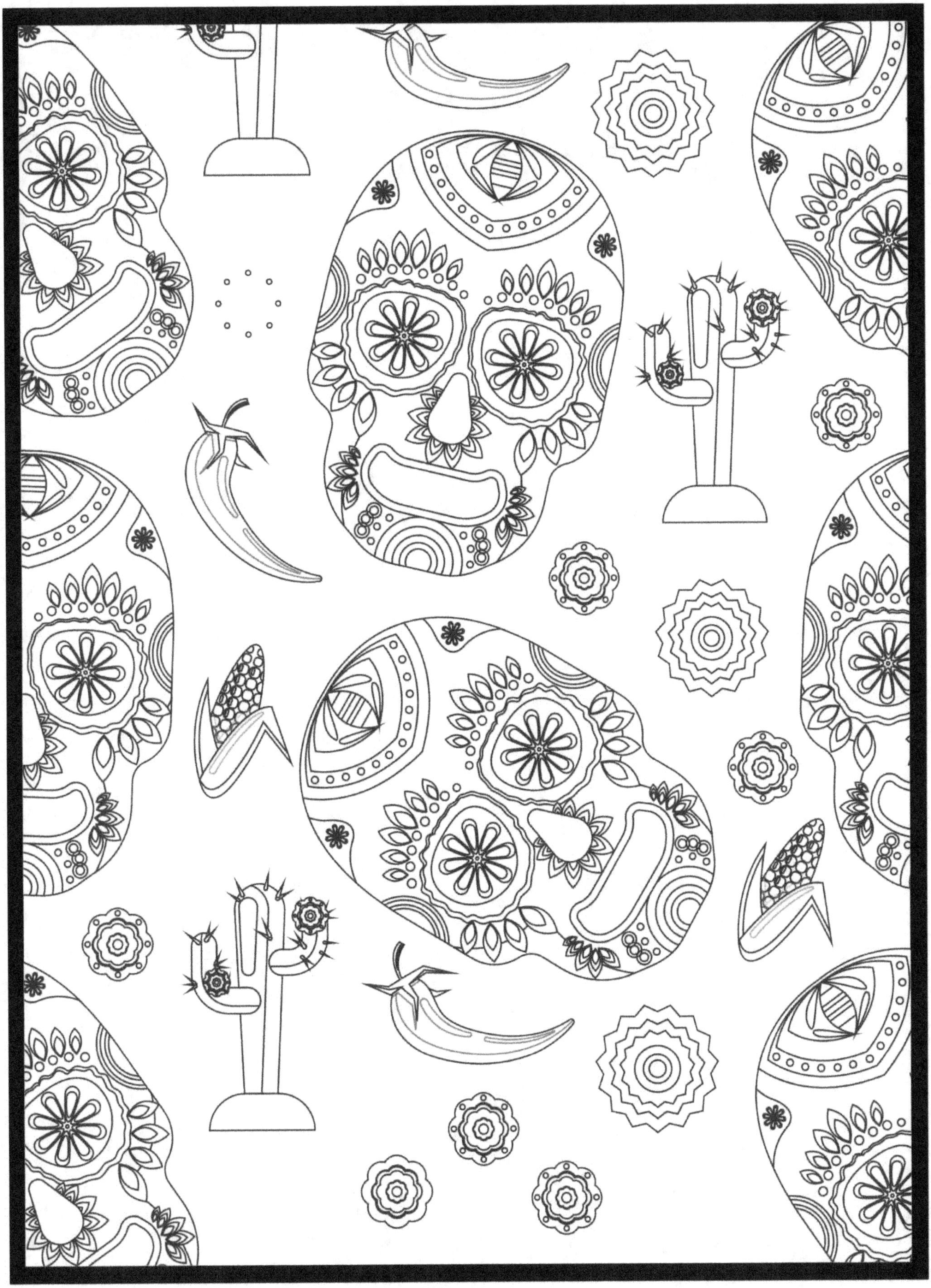

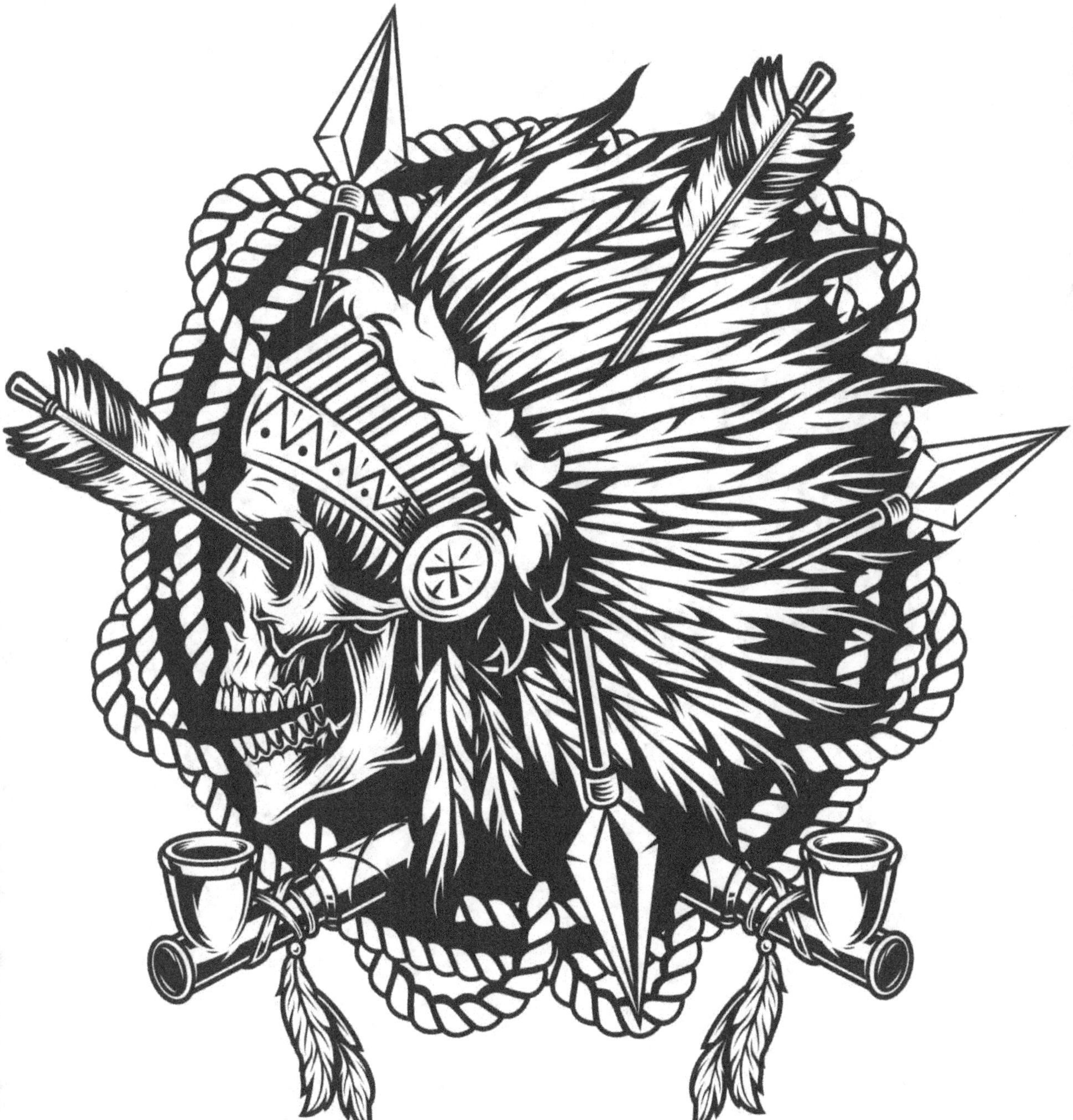

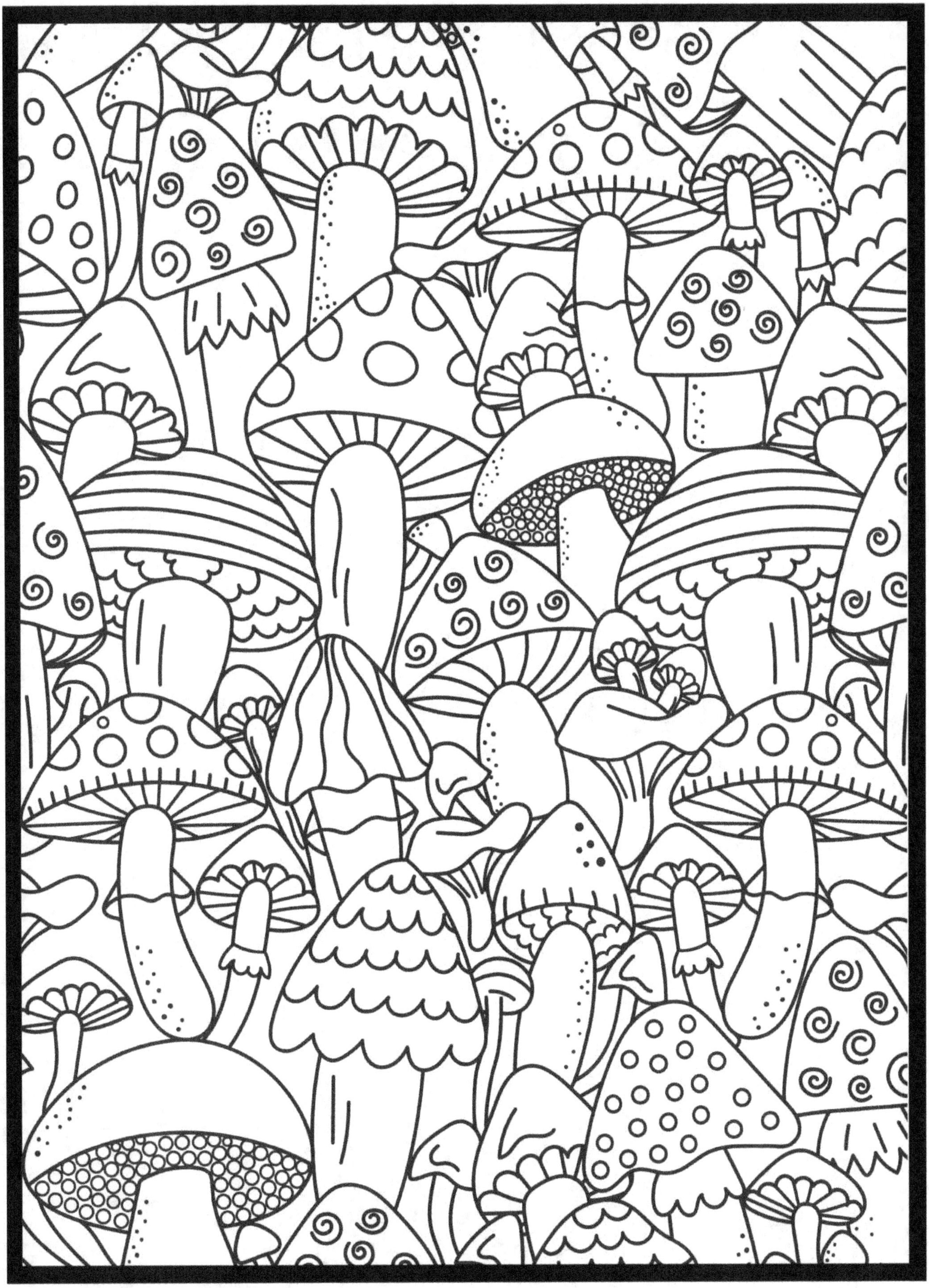

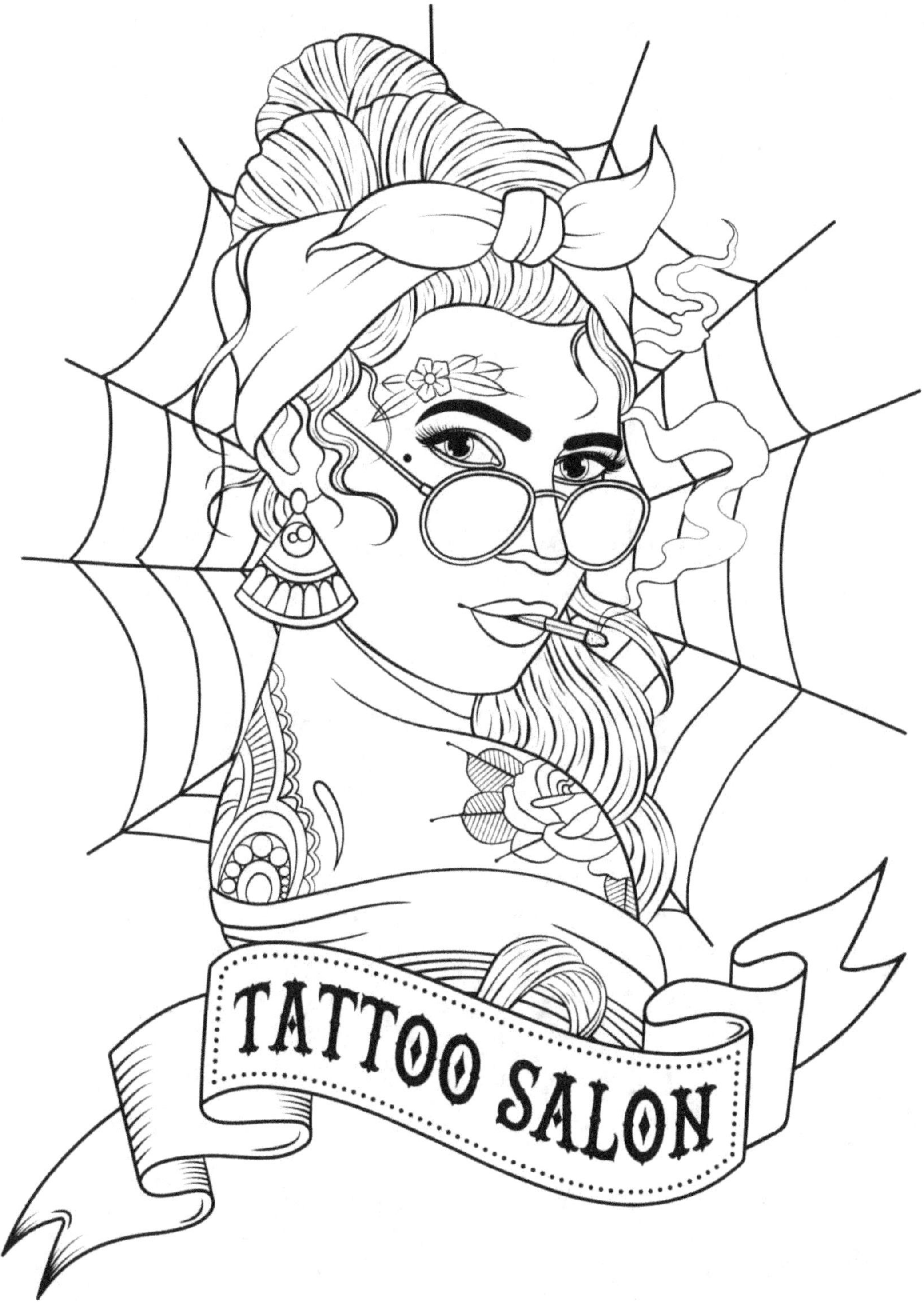
TATTOO SALON

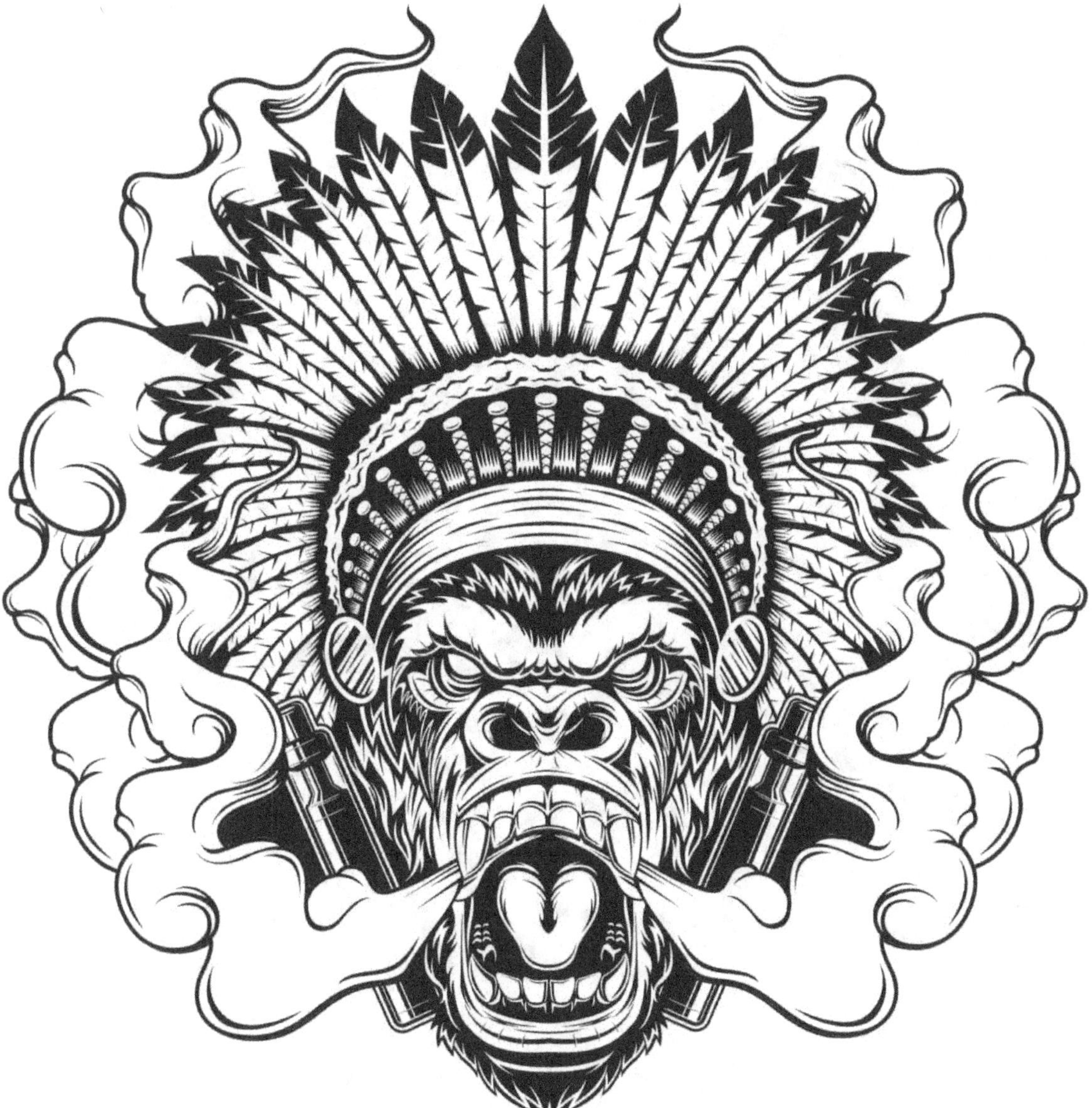

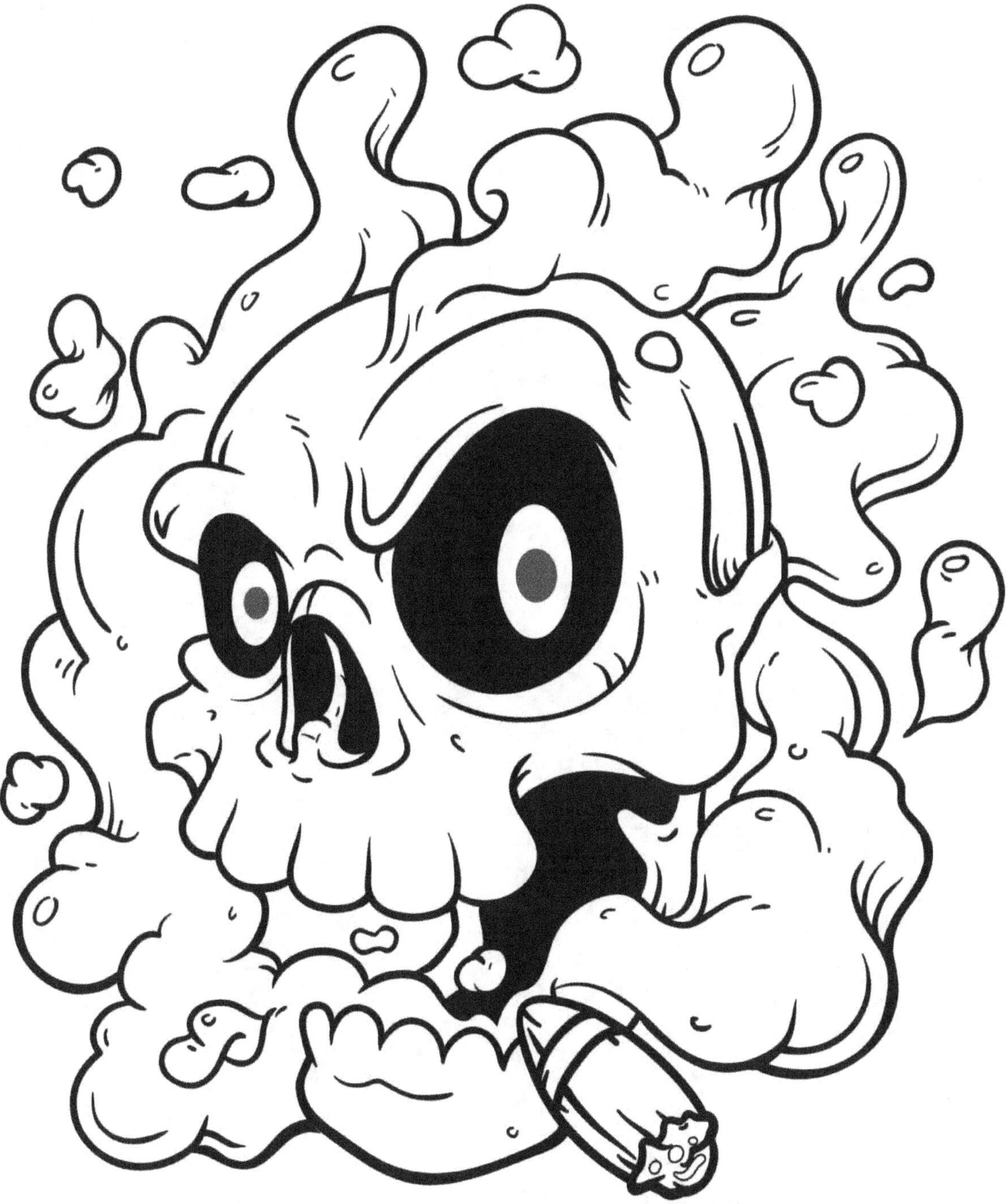

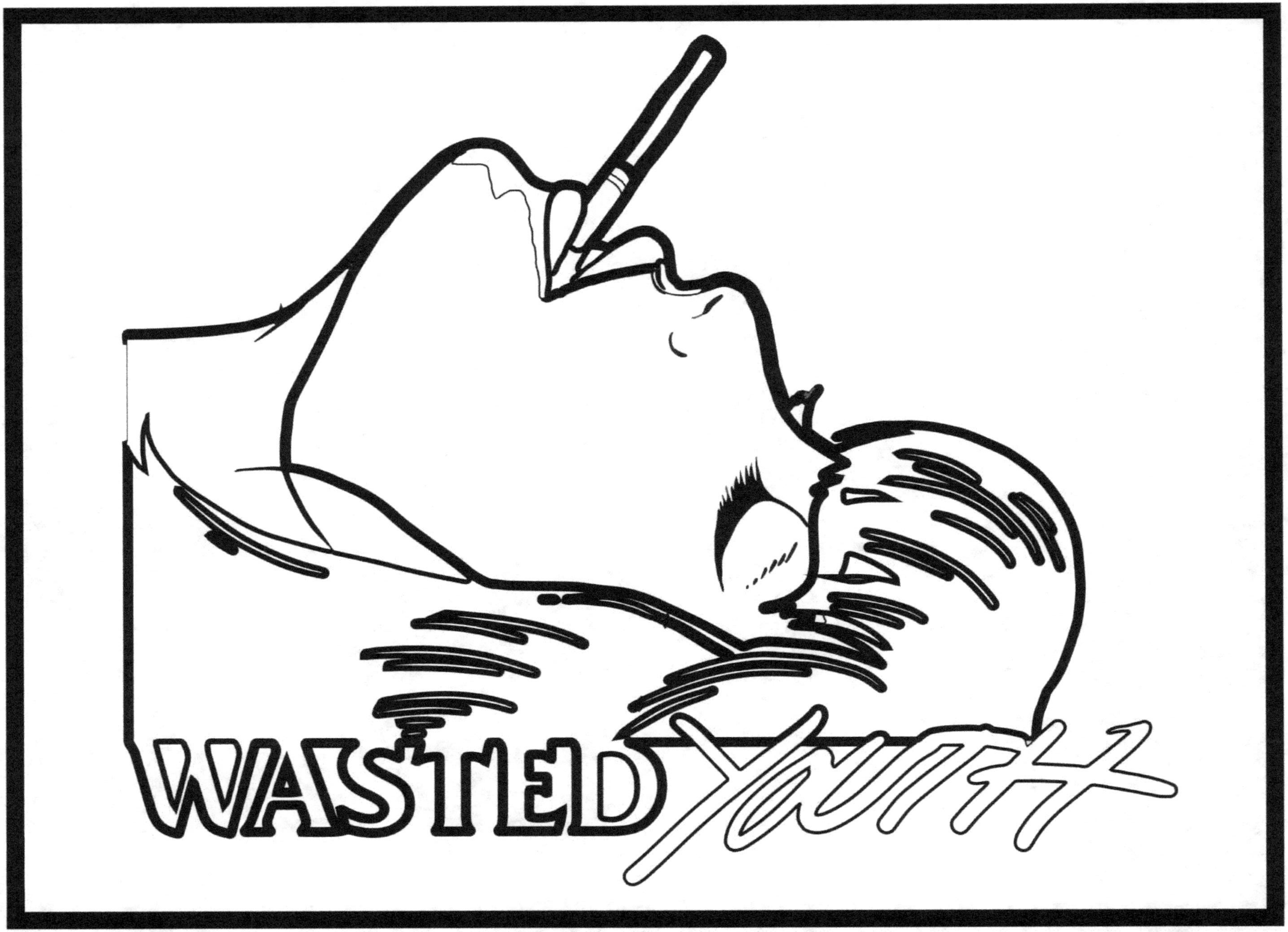
WASTED Youth

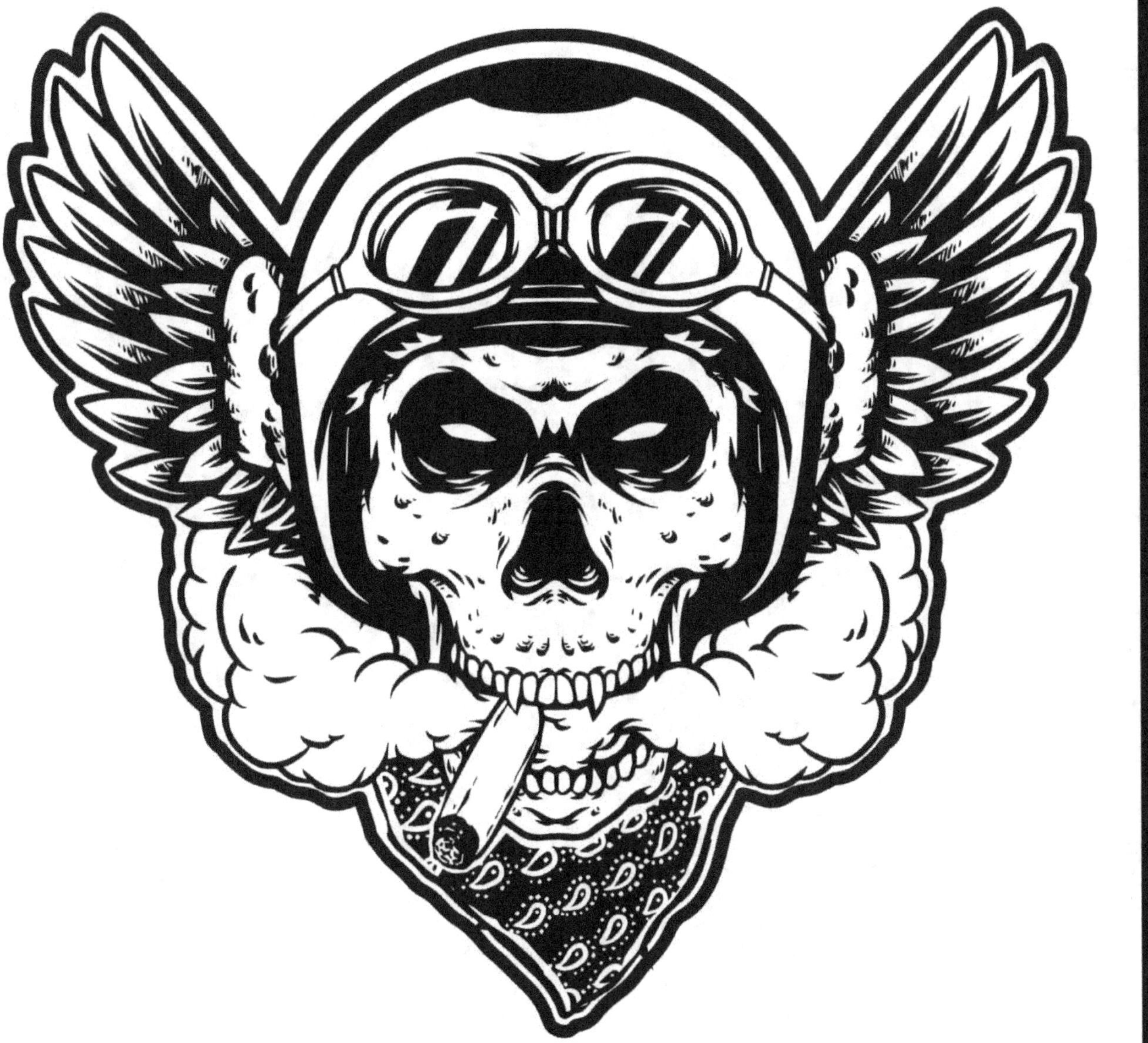

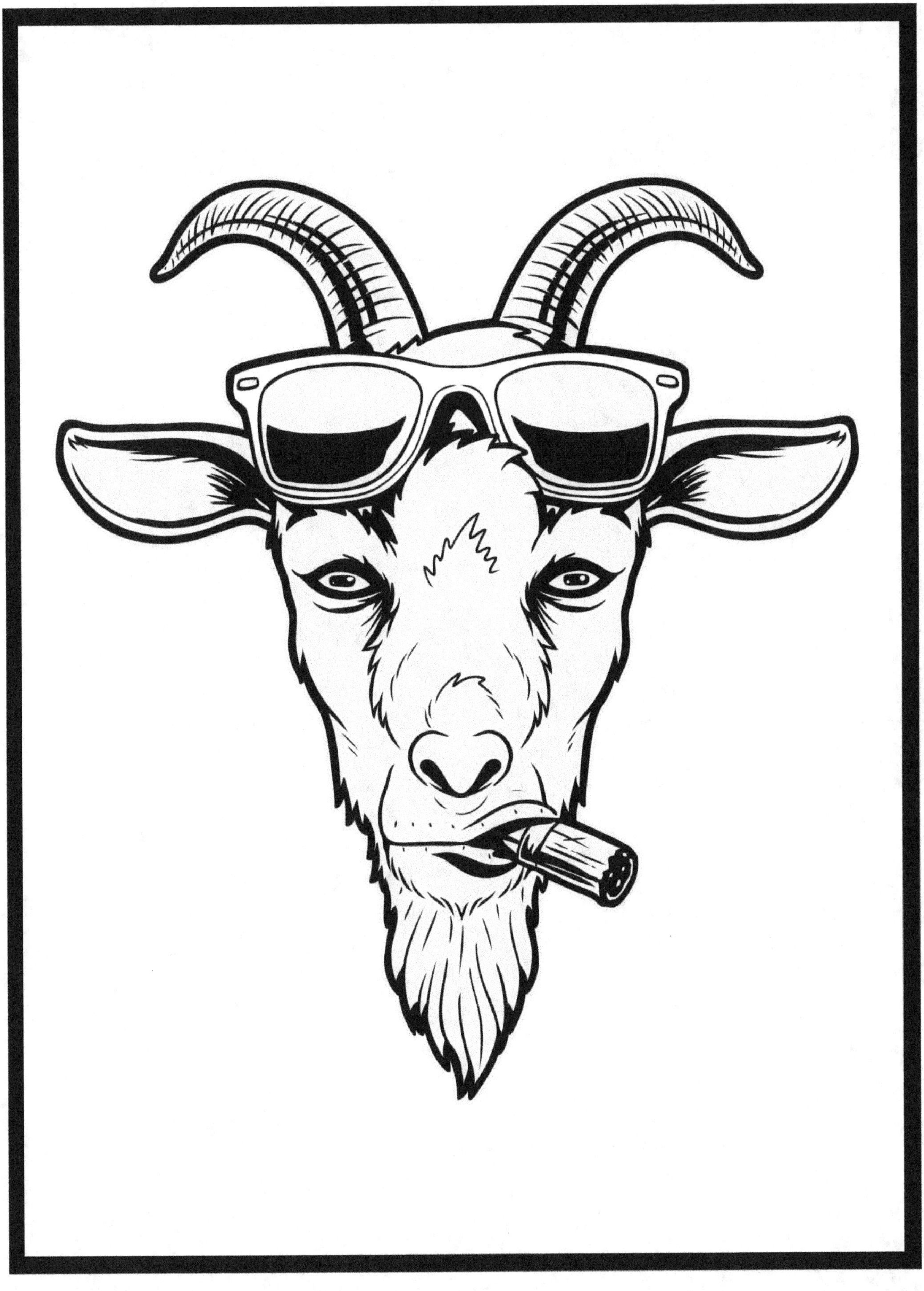

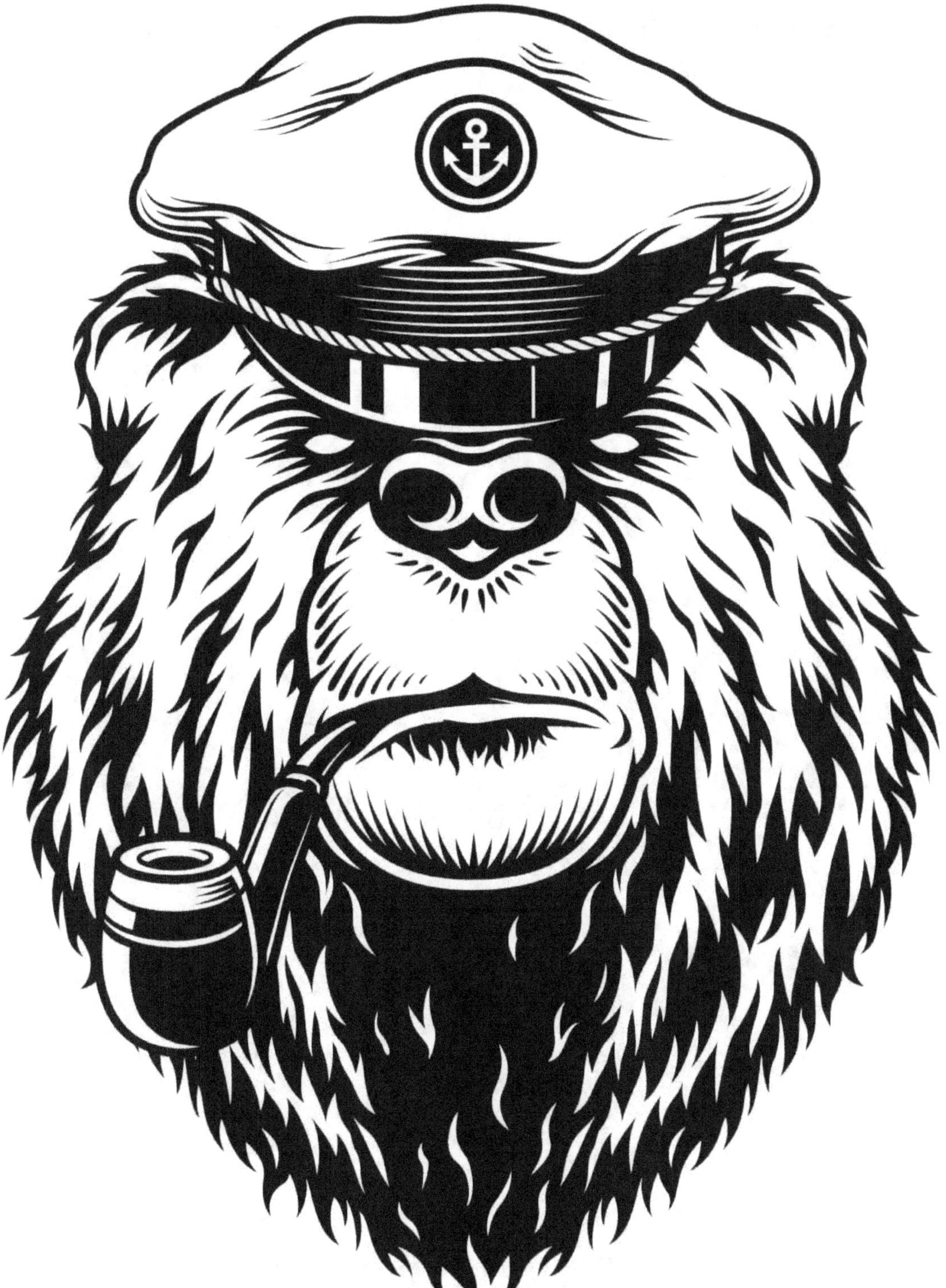

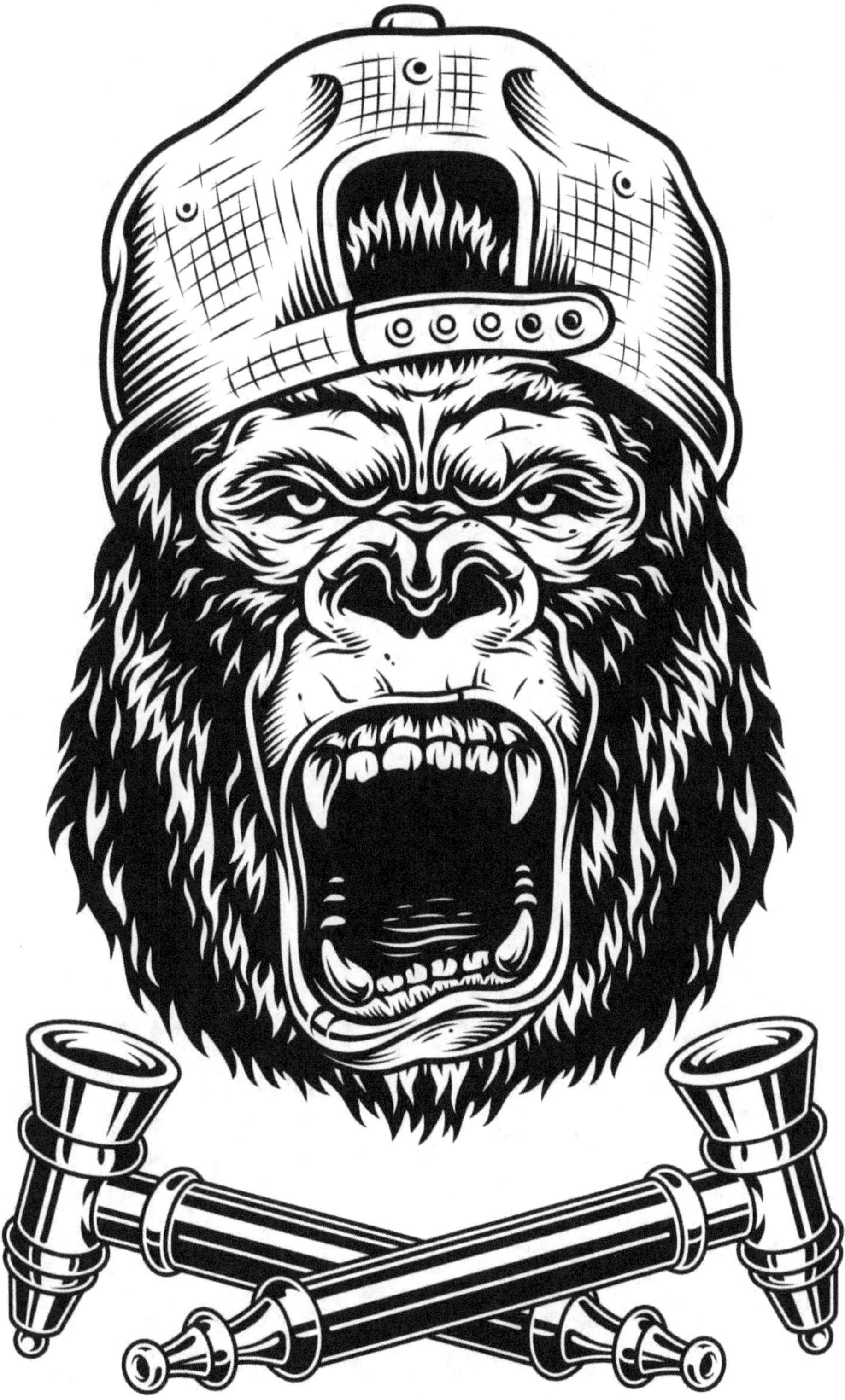

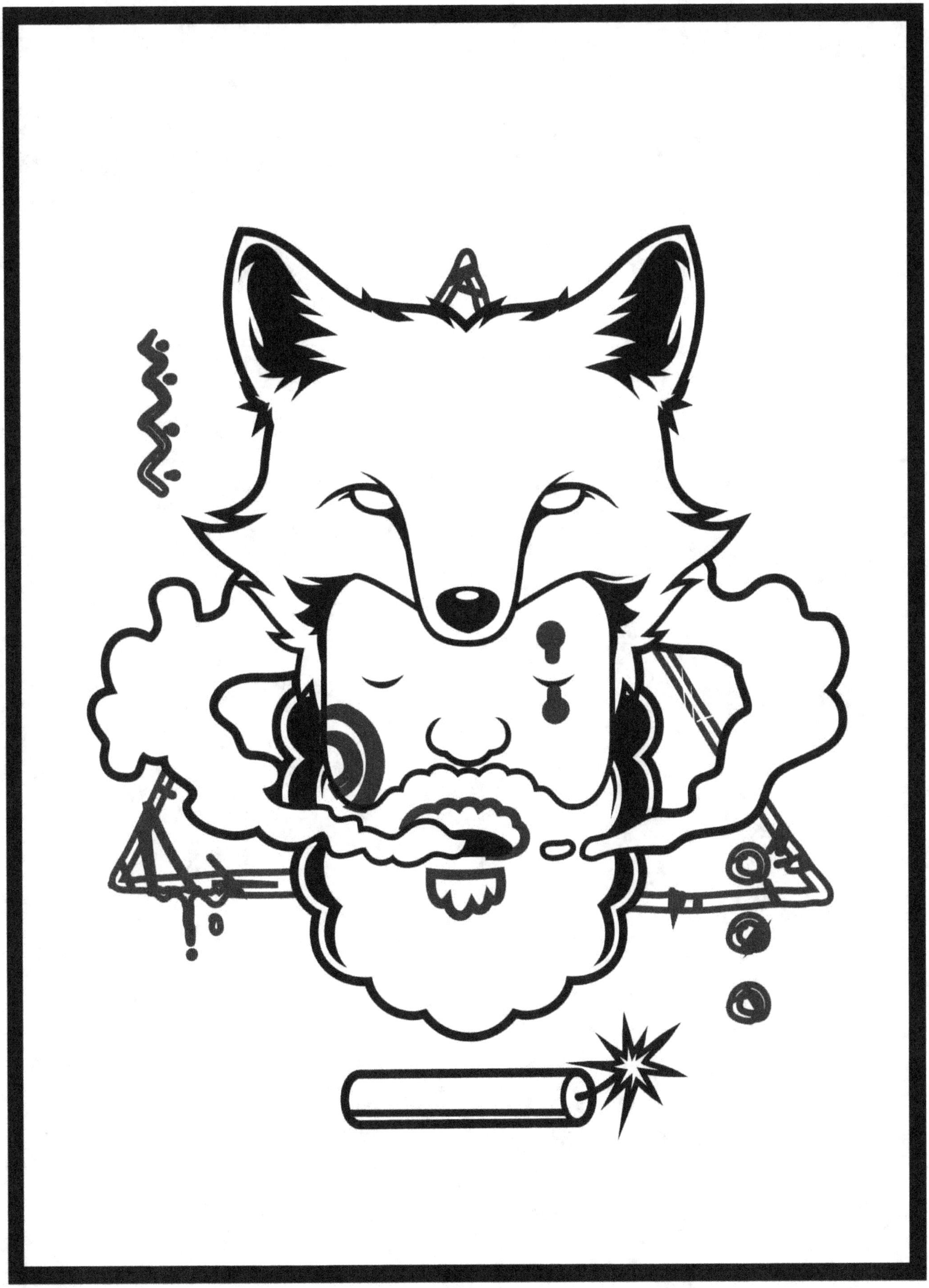

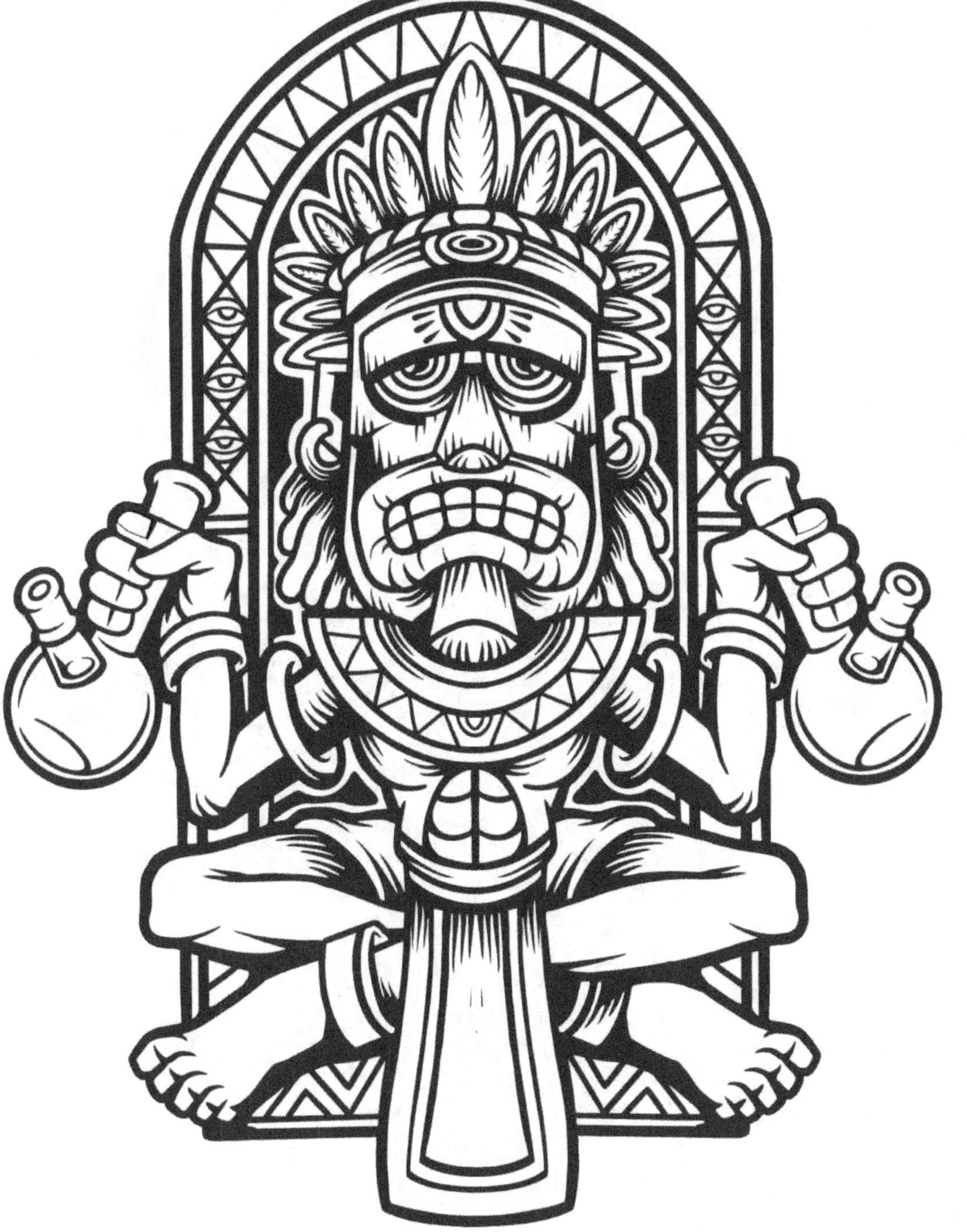

www.ingramcontent.com/pod-product-compliance
Lightning Source LLC
Chambersburg PA
CBHW080508220526
45465CB00006B/2415
* 9 7 9 8 6 6 3 9 7 9 5 3 5 *